# Daniel

The Key to Prophecy

Darrin Yeager

---
Frames of Reference LLC

# Daniel
The Key to Prophecy

Copyright © 2023 Darrin Yeager
All rights reserved. No part of this book may be reproduced in any form, known now or in the future, without written permission of the copyright owner, except for brief quotations in reviews or other materials.

https://www.dyeager.org/

$\int_\alpha^\Omega$ ISBN 978-0-9831117-8-8
Published by Frames of Reference LLC

The integral sign with alpha and omega limits logo is a trademark of Frames of Reference LLC.
Unless otherwise noted, Bible passages are from the King James Version of the Bible.
Passages marked NKJV taken from the New King James Version of the Bible copyright ©1979, 1980, 1982 by Thomas Nelson Inc. Used by permission. All rights reserved.
Scripture quotations marked New Living Translation (NLT) are taken from the Holy Bible, New Living Translation, copyright © 1996. Used by permission of Tyndale House Publishers, Inc., Wheaton, Illinois 60189. All rights reserved.
31 27 09 20 03

# Table of Contents

| | | |
|---|---|---|
| 1 | Introduction | 1 |
| 2 | Chapter One | 9 |
| 3 | Chapter Two | 17 |
| 4 | Chapter Three | 35 |
| 5 | Chapter Four | 55 |
| 6 | Chapter Five | 67 |
| 7 | Chapter Six | 81 |
| 8 | Chapter Seven | 93 |
| 9 | Chapter Eight | 103 |
| 10 | Seventy Weeks of Daniel | 113 |
| 11 | Chapter Nine | 123 |
| 12 | Chapter Ten | 137 |
| 13 | Chapter Eleven | 145 |
| 14 | Chapter Twelve | 155 |
| A | The Confusion of Religion | 161 |
| | References | 167 |

## Chapter 1

## Introduction

EVEN THOUGH DANIEL WROTE thousands of years ago, his book provides clarity and relevance today — a prophetic book you need to understand as it forms the foundation for all prophecy. In the middle of Jesus' private briefing to His disciples on the end of the age (Matthew 24), Matthew inserts a parenthetical statement — "Let the reader understand" — you should understand Daniel for the clarity and understanding it provides current events.

Yet people fear Daniel's book (and Revelation), viewing end times as scary, fearful events, but they should not be. God provides knowledge for a reason — if He didn't want us to understand, He would not have revealed it.

On the other side, others devote too much time to prophecy, derailing more profitable studies. Each time war breaks out in the Middle East "experts" appear debating on whether it's the beginning of Armageddon. Who cares? Yes, we should know and understand times and events, but not devote unreasonable amounts of time; we don't know if any specific event triggers the final week of Daniel's prophecy, so understand but don't obsess.

Likewise, it's easy to fall into the trap we *do* understand how prophecy plays out. You might recall hearing a teacher speak on Daniel and the abomination of desolation and how everyone will see it. The commentator said something like "see, this was impossible before the age of satellite television, but today it's easy."

Those were common comments in the '60s and '70s. Today? Laughable. Ever hear of this new-fangled thing called the Internet? YouTube? Even today, YouTube and Internet might not be how Daniel's prophecy plays out, so don't focus on a singular idea, but keep an open mind.

Daniel's writing thousands of years ago provides euphemisms still in use today (even in secular circles):

- "handwriting on the wall"
- "your numbers up"
- "idol has clay feet"
- "thrown to the lions"

Daniel's prophecy and narratives provide abundant learning opportunities — not as stories for entertainment, but events which should change our actions.

*For whatever things were written in earlier times were written for our learning, that we through patience and comfort of the scriptures might have hope.* Romans 15:4

Daniel provides the antidote for one large heresy today — God no longer involves the Jews in His plan. Some teach since the Jews didn't accept their Messiah the promises made to Abraham transferred to the church; the Church replaced the Jews in Bible prophecy. Is this scriptural? Does the Bible contain *any* such teaching? Never — the promises made in Genesis are *unilateral* and *irrevocable*:

*And I will bless them that bless thee, and curse him that curseth thee.* Genesis 12:3

That's an idea we need to understand as we muddle around with foreign policy (and a promise still in effect which should guide how we handle the Middle East mess). It's bizarre to imagine, but the creator of the universe reserved a tract of land He calls His own — God's covenant with Abraham in Genesis 15:1-18 is unilateral.

*And he said unto him, I am the LORD that brought thee out of Ur of the Chaldees, to give thee this land to inherit it. And he said, Lord GOD, whereby shall I know that I shall inherit it? And he said unto him, Take me an heifer of three years old, and a she goat of three years old, and a ram of three years old, and a turtledove, and a young pigeon. And he took unto him all these, and divided them in the midst, and laid each piece one against another: but the birds divided he not. And when the fowls came down upon the carcases, Abram drove them away. And when the sun was going down, a deep sleep fell upon Abram; and, lo, an horror of great darkness fell upon him.*

# Introduction

*And it came to pass, that, when the sun went down, and it was dark, behold a smoking furnace, and a burning lamp that passed between those pieces. In the same day the LORD made a covenant with Abram, saying, Unto thy seed have I given this land, from the river of Egypt unto the great river, the river Euphrates.*
Genesis 15:7-12,17-18

Parties formed a contract by dividing an animal in half, with both parties passing between the pieces to seal the deal. Since Abraham fell asleep, he never fulfilled his part as God passed through by Himself — Abraham received a unilateral and irrevocable contract from God alone. By itself the contract establishes the certainty of the Jewish future, but consider Daniel and the famous seventy weeks.

*Seventy weeks are determined upon thy people and upon thy holy city, to finish the transgression, and to make an end of sins, and to make reconciliation for iniquity, and to bring in everlasting righteousness, and to seal up the vision and prophecy, and to anoint the most Holy.*
Daniel 9:24

Two facts become immediately and obviously clear by even a casual reading of that passage.

1. It's about the Jews — "thy people and thy holy city." Daniel's seventy weeks involves Jewish history, not Gentile.
2. It hasn't happened yet — finishing transgression, the end of sins, reconciliation for iniquity, and everlasting righteousness.

The Jews have a future yet to be revealed. Currently we're in the interval between the $69^{th}$ and $70^{th}$ week; while Daniel speaks of all end times, he doesn't include much detail; Revelation fills in events of the $70^{th}$ week.

Daniel means "God is my judge." Daniel began captivity in Babylon early in his teen years under Nebuchadnezzar, spending most of his life in Babylon. As to the date of his writing, critics try to "late-date" the book to the second century BC, and not by Daniel's pen as the clarity (and obviously fulfilled) nature of the prophecies demand skeptics to insist no man could be so accurate regarding future events; they favor a date around 165 BC, by an author other than Daniel.

> *Although according to the text the book of Daniel belongs to the 6<sup>th</sup> century BC, most scholars do not believe the book was written then. They opt for a 2<sup>nd</sup> century BC writer, drawing on well-known stories.\**

Notice the use of the terms "believe" and "opt" — even the terms hint of their refusal to believe Daniel foretold future events. Since they begin with a preconceived bias of doubting God's existence, the only other possibility denies Daniel's authorship, and not during the time the events took place. Is this so-called "modern scholarship" correct? They may have PhDs, fancy titles, and sound intelligent, but are they right? They choose to ignore historical facts.

1. Alexander the Great visits Jerusalem in 332 BC. The historian Josephus† relates a story of Alexander in Jerusalem as they showed him a copy of Daniel. Thus, it had to exist in 332 BC. Alexander dies in 323 BC so even if the Jerusalem date is off a bit, Daniel's writing *had* to exist before 323 BC.

2. The completion of the Septuagint (Greek translation of the Hebrew Old Testament) occurred about 285–246 BC.

Again, scholars debate exact dates, but let's approximate to the middle of the third century and round off to the period 300-200 BC. Since the Old Testament contains Daniel (and included in the Septuagint), it's impossible for the writing to be as late as 165 BC.

Both historical events shred "scholarship" stating the book bearing Daniel's name wasn't written as claimed, but much later — you don't have to examine their arguments (no matter how scholarly sounding) to dismiss them. They waste years debating arguments which can not be true due to historical events. By continuing to hold meritless theories, they discredit themselves from serious consideration.

If a later forger wrote Daniel, the Septuagint doesn't exist (or at least was completed much later), and neither did Alexander's visit to Jerusalem. Interestingly, you can find "scholarship" doubting both events — not because it makes sense, but because it must be to fit preconceived ideas regarding Daniel's writing. Be careful with "scholars" sounding sophisticated; they attempt to cause

---

\*     Alexander (1999, page 473)
†     Josephus (1987, Book 11, chapter 8, section 5)

# Introduction

doubt even though they ignore facts rendering their scholarship in error. Let's boil it down to J Vernon McGee's notes:

> *These arguments clearly contradict the liberal critics; yet there are those who blindly ignore them. It is not in the purview of these brief comments to enter into useless argument and fight again about that which has already been settled ... that the man Daniel was not a deceiver and that his book was not a forgery.*[*]

Let's skip the pseudo-scholarship and settle the matter once and for all — in Matthew 24:5 Jesus declares "When ye therefore shall see the abomination of desolation, *spoken of by Daniel the prophet*," providing two insights: Daniel authored the book bearing his name, and he was a prophet. If the Bible is the inerrant Word of God it settles the authorship and date of Daniel (if you don't believe Jesus is God then you should address bigger issues than the authorship of Daniel).

Anyone claiming a forger wrote Daniel in 165 BC tells you they deny the inerrancy of God's Word, and don't believe Jesus is God. That doesn't immediately discredit their theories, but it should show insight into their bias and show you no matter what their scholarship says, it builds from a foundation of preconceived bias and a closed mind.

> *The endorsement of the Lord Jesus Christ is valid and sufficient for every believer, whether or not he has examined the arguments of the critics, and it satisfies the sincere saint without his having to study the answers of conservative scholarship.*[†]

Thus Daniel wrote between 605 BC and 537 BC during captivity in Babylon. Carried off as a captive early in his teen years, he lived and wrote during that time. He spent much of his life in service to the government of Babylon, receiving incredible prophecies and revelations from God.

The theme of Daniel's life appears early in chapter 1 with Daniel saying he "purposed in his heart not to defile himself." Even as a young teenager far from home, Daniel maintained devotion to God; Daniel refused to defile himself in several ways.

---

[*] McGee (1982, page 525)
[†] McGee (1982, page 525)

- With Food (1:8) — He stayed kosher to Jewish law. Who would know if he ate a ham sandwich? He's in Babylon with nobody around to know otherwise.
- From Fear (2:16–18) — After none of the other officials could tell Nebuchadnezzar his dream, the king places the entire group under death penalty for failure to perform. But Daniel prays to God for understanding of Nebuchadnezzar's dream and reveals to the King not only the dream, but its interpretation.
- Power/gifts (5:17) — After he interprets the handwriting on the wall, the king desires to give gifts and third place in the kingdom to Daniel, but he tells the king "Let thy gifts be to thyself, and give thy rewards to another"; Daniel doesn't change by influence of money or power.
- From corrupt laws (6:5–7) — A law made no petitions legal for thirty days to any god or man but the King (a law created specifically to trap Daniel). Yet he refuses to yield, and God protects him in the lion's den.

We can sum up the character of Daniel from chapter 6.

*Then this Daniel was preferred above the presidents and princes, because an excellent spirit was in him; and the king thought to set him over the whole realm. Then the presidents and princes sought to find occasion against Daniel concerning the kingdom; but they could find none occasion nor fault; forasmuch as he was faithful, neither was there any error or fault found in him. Then said these men, We shall not find any occasion against this Daniel, except we find it against him concerning the law of his God.* Daniel 6:3–5

Daniel's closet contained no skeletons; no way to attack him for "youthful indiscretions," "wardrobe malfunctions," or anything else. The *only* path to attack Daniel came from his devotion to God; as the book shows from youth to old age, Daniel refused to compromise.

Contrast Daniel's commitment with today — Daniel refused to defile himself even though nobody watched; would anybody care if he devoured a ham sandwich? Would anybody even know? People today scorn and ignore Daniel's model; people corrupt themselves *because* people watch, after all, bad publicity is better than none, so they say.

It's a race to the bottom, not because no morals or ethics exist (though a strong possibility), but because it's all good publicity.

# Introduction

In this disastrous race, it's only a race to the bottom as each tries to top the other by sinking to previously unheard of depths. Truly, our society slouches toward Gomorrah.

Yet Daniel maintains his character even though no one expected (or cared) him to. You could imagine other government officials didn't like Daniel (or his integrity), so they set a trap stating for thirty days no one could petition any god or man but the king — and Daniel responds.

> *Now when Daniel knew that the writing was signed, he went into his house; and his windows being open in his chamber toward Jerusalem, he kneeled upon his knees three times a day, and prayed, and gave thanks before his God, as he did previously.*     Daniel 6:10

Daniel possesses mind over matter — he didn't mind whatever trap, law, or roadblock appeared in his path, so they don't matter. Sadly his example isn't followed much today.

You've seen the martyr complex; anytime a new rule or law appears, they screech "persecution" and look to sue, evade, or score political points (instead of ministry, which doesn't make the to-do list). Sadly, pastors easily fall into this trap; those doing so should retire and form a political action group.

A statement impossible to over-emphasize: politics has *nothing* to do with the church or its mission. Nothing. Nada. Zip. Zero. *Principles* certainly do (as Daniel shows), but political rocks are generally better left unturned, at least as far as the church and pastors are concerned.

The dawn of the pandemic era (2019–2021) found pastors falling into this error, trading ministry for politics. If you scanned news from the period, you noticed pastors proudly and boldly abandoning their mission for politics, lawsuits, and divisive behavior, walking away from the fruit of the spirit for the fruit of the flesh — hostility, quarreling, jealousy, outbursts of anger, selfish ambition, dissension, division...*

Why many pastors willfully and proudly abandoned their posts for politics might be the biggest mystery of the age.

The history of the church demonstrates it and its pastors never learn from lessons of the past, and instead of repairing and repenting for past divisions, instead create new ones. Emo Phillips has been identified as the author of the following joke, and like most humor, it's funny (and sad) because it's so true.

---

\*    Galatians 5 NLT

*Once I saw this guy on a bridge about to jump. I said, "Don't do it!"*

*He said, "Nobody loves me."*

*I said, "God loves you. Do you believe in God?"*

*He said, "Yes." I said, "Are you a Christian or a Jew?"*

*He said, "A Christian." I said, "Me, too! Protestant or Catholic?"*

*He said, "Protestant." I said, "Me, too! What franchise?"*

*He said, "Baptist." I said, "Me, too!*

*Northern Baptist or Southern Baptist?" He said, "Northern Baptist." I said, "Me, too!*

*Northern Conservative Baptist or Northern Liberal Baptist?" He said, "Northern Conservative Baptist." I said, "Me, too!*

*Northern Conservative Baptist Great Lakes Region, or Northern Conservative Baptist Eastern Region?" He said, "Northern Conservative Baptist Great Lakes Region." I said, "Me, too!"*

*"Northern Conservative Baptist Great Lakes Region Council of 1879, or Northern Conservative Baptist Great Lakes Region Council of 1912?" He said, "Northern Conservative Baptist Great Lakes Region Council of 1912."*

*I said, "Die, heretic!" And I pushed him over.*

Baptism. Pre-Trib. Calvinism. Bible translations. Sadly, the dawn of the pandemic age showed the church isn't finished adding to the list it will divide over, and pastors willfully abandoning their ministry post, trading it for divisive and trivial political or non-doctrinal issues.

Think about what you do before you do it. It should be that simple, but the pandemic age proved pastors aren't immune from failure to use critical thinking and logic, wandering way off course. Thou shalt not tempt the Lord thy God. He gave you a brain to think and analyze. Use it.

What do we learn from Daniel? As they set a trap *specifically for Daniel* he didn't pay much attention — he neither screeched persecution and threatened lawsuits, nor did he hide. He continued as he always did, *knowing the consequences of doing so could be severe.*

Daniel's character — bold, dedicated, uncompromising, and refusing to defile himself.

*Chapter 2*

# Chapter One

*In the third year of the reign of Jehoiakim king of Judah came Nebuchadnezzar king of Babylon unto Jerusalem, and besieged it. And the Lord gave Jehoiakim king of Judah into his hand, with part of the vessels of the house of God, which he carried into the land of Shinar to the house of his god; and he brought the vessels into the treasure house of his god.*

Daniel 1:1–2

Nebuchadnezzar ruled from 605–562 BC, placing Jehoiakim as vassal king after his first siege of Jerusalem and returned to Babylon. Unfortunately, after three years Jehoiakim listens to false prophets claiming God will deliver Jerusalem from Nebuchadnezzar, thus Jehoiakim rebels against Nebuchadnezzar (2 Kings 24:1, 2 Chronicles 36:1-8). God allowed Nebuchadnezzar to take Jerusalem for His reasons — a warning for people thinking God will always give you an easy life with a Lexus, ice cream, and a pony. Consider Jeremiah 27–29 for a warning against listening only to people who tell you what you want to hear.

*And it came to pass the same year, in the beginning of the reign of Zedekiah king of Judah, in the fourth year, and in the fifth month, that Hananiah the son of Azur the prophet, which was of Gibeon, spoke unto me in the house of the Lord, in the presence of the priests and of all the people, saying, Thus speaketh the Lord of hosts, the God of Israel, saying, I have broken the yoke of the king of Babylon. Within two full years will I bring again into this place all the vessels of the Lord's house, that Nebuchadnezzar king of Babylon took away from this place, and carried them to Babylon; And I will bring again to this place Jeconiah the son of Jehoiakim king of Judah, with all the captives of Judah, that went into Babylon, saith the Lord; for I will break the yoke of the king of Babylon.*

*Then the prophet Jeremiah said unto the prophet Hananiah in the presence of the priests, and in the presence of all the people that stood in the house of the Lord, Even the prophet Jeremiah said, Amen! The Lord do so; the Lord perform thy words which thou hast prophesied, to bring again the vessels of the Lord's house, and all that is carried away captive, from Babylon into this place. Nevertheless hear thou now this word that I speak in thine ears, and in the ears of all the people; The prophets that have been before me and before thee of old prophesied both against many countries, and against great kingdoms, of war, and of evil, and of pestilence. The prophet which prophesieth of peace, when the word of the prophet shall come to pass, then shall the prophet be known, that the Lord hath truly sent him.*

*Then Hananiah the prophet took the yoke from off the prophet Jeremiah's neck, and broke it. And Hananiah spoke in the presence of all the people, saying, Thus saith the Lord; Even so will I break the yoke of Nebuchadnezzar king of Babylon from the neck of all nations within the space of two full years. And the prophet Jeremiah went his way.*

*Then the word of the Lord came unto Jeremiah the prophet, after that Hananiah the prophet had broken the yoke from off the neck of the prophet Jeremiah, saying, Go and tell Hananiah, saying, Thus saith the Lord; Thou hast broken the yokes of wood; but thou shalt make for them yokes of iron. For thus saith the Lord of hosts, the God of Israel; I have put a yoke of iron upon the neck of all these nations, that they may serve Nebuchadnezzar king of Babylon; and they shall serve him; and I have given him the beasts of the field also.*

*Then said the prophet Jeremiah unto Hananiah the prophet, Hear now, Hananiah; The Lord hath not sent thee; but thou makest this people to trust in a lie. Therefore thus saith the Lord; Behold, I will cast thee from off the face of the earth; this year thou shalt die, because thou hast taught rebellion against the Lord. So Hananiah the prophet died the same year in the seventh month.* Jeremiah 28

Who gave Nebuchadnezzar Jerusalem? The Lord did. God delivered the people into captivity for a reason; when God says it, believe it. He uses different events as His judgment and tools, yet it wasn't popular so prophets arrive telling the king what he wants to hear — the captivity will end if you rebel against Nebuchadnezzar. Unfortunately, Jehoiakim listened to the false prophets; you must beware of people telling you what you want to hear.

We're not as foolish as the kings of old? Nope. Pastors replacing truth with populism discover a quick way to increase attendance (and $$$), telling the people what they want to hear, politically or religiously. Nothing changed during thousands of years, as Paul warns Timothy.

*For the time will come when they will not endure sound doctrine; but after their own lusts shall they heap to themselves teachers, having itching ears; And they shall turn away their ears from the truth, and shall be turned unto fables.*
2 Timothy 4:3–4

At the dawn of the pandemic age (2019–2021) Paul's words ring clearer than ever. For unknown reasons Christians stumble toward anti-science delusion, listening to people lacking qualifications to speak on what they pontificate on — a list including pastors — and prefer to hear what tickles their ears instead of facts and reason. Joining the pastorate does *not* instantly confer expertise on math or science, and when a pastor wanders off into areas they lack expertise on their members suffer for it.

Spouting ridiculous anti-science ideas will *always* be not only unwise, but ungodly and heretical.

What? — those are strong words. God is a god of reason, logic, and order; it's *why* the scientific method works (i.e. make a guess, perform experiments to prove or disprove the guess, and modify your ideas based on real data). If a Christian proclaims anti-science views (don't trust it, it doesn't work, etc) it proves they reject everything the Bible teaches.

They may not *state* it as such, but rejecting logic, order, and thinking skills rejects the world God created. Arguing God made a mistake might be the worst form of pride, a sin causing a certain angel quite a bit of trouble.

*How art thou fallen from heaven, O Lucifer, son of the morning! How art thou cut down to the ground, which didst weaken the nations! For thou hast said in thine heart, I will ascend into heaven, I will exalt my throne above the stars of God: I will sit also upon the mount of the congregation, in the sides of*

> *the north; I will ascend above the heights of the clouds; I will be like the most High.*
> 
> Isaiah 14:12—14

Don't call God a liar or mistaken; claiming science fails and you know better than God duplicates the *exact* mistake of Satan, saying "move over God, I've got this." No, you don't; trust the order and logic God created. Science works *because* God is a god of order, logic, and reason. God gave you a brain and ability to reason, use it.

God's truth never wins popularity contests, either in Daniel's time or today. False prophets told the king God would deliver them from Nebuchadnezzar. But perhaps something needs to be learned, perhaps a lesson you can't (or won't) learn any other way. As your physical body needs exercise (which isn't fun), your spiritual body requires the benefits of something which isn't much fun to go through.

It's easier to believe God will *always* deliver you from a tough spot, but it's not true. Many churches become popular telling people what they want to hear (instead of proclaiming God's Word), doing a great disservice to people — if you're not healed, or rich, or obtain the promotion, it's because you didn't have enough faith. Is that Biblical? I think not — Paul prayed three times for the removal of his thorn in the flesh, and it wasn't (if he lacked faith, I sure wouldn't want the assignment informing him).

Why does God deliver some and not others? I don't know. We do know God values spiritual principles superior to physical items; we hold the opposite view. It's popular to point to the book of Job as an example — but the lesson of Job isn't why the innocent suffer, but the need for the divine viewpoint (Job 38:4–6, 40:8–9) as God calls Job and asks "who are you to question me?" A question Job can't answer (neither can we). As Bill Ritchie says, "if God is God, then God is God." Leave the reason to God, your task is to trust Him.

> *And the king spoke unto Ashpenaz the master of his eunuchs, that he should bring certain of the children of Israel, and of the king's seed, and of the princes; Youths in whom was no blemish, but well favored, and skillful in all wisdom, and gifted in knowledge, and understanding science, and such as had ability in them to stand in the king's palace, and whom they might teach the learning and the tongue of the Chaldeans.*
> 
> Daniel 1:3–4

## Chapter One

Nebuchadnezzar desires the best of the captives to serve in the government, providing years of schooling to discern the best before they serve the king. This was common during this time — smart conquerors utilizing skills of the conquered.

Daniel was as young as fourteen, but could have been as old as nineteen (we'll approximate and call him a teenager). Imagine being taken as a youth far away where you knew no one. Could you maintain your dedication? After all, who would know? No photos would appear on the Internet, and nobody expects you to maintain your devotion. It would be challenging to maintain your devotion in a situation where nobody cared, and nobody would know if you failed to follow Jewish law.

Daniel receives years of training from the best the king could offer; he was intelligent and well-schooled by the best the empire had. It's popular to cast religious people as uninformed dummies, only after being enlightened do you realize the sham of religion and come to true knowledge. Daniel was the best and brightest with considerable training, serving under several kings as an excellent administrator.

*And the king appointed them a daily provision of the king's food, and of the wine which he drank, so nourishing them three years, that at the end thereof they might stand before the king.*
Daniel 1:5

Daniel received good food — not prisoner rations. Nebuchadnezzar treated them well with schooling and food, a contrast to other kings who after conquering an area didn't treat people so well. Nebuchadnezzar desired to improve his government by utilizing skills of people he conquered.

*Now among these were of the children of Judah, Daniel, Hananiah, Mishael, and Azariah, Unto whom the prince of the eunuchs gave names; for he gave unto Daniel the name of Belteshazzar; and to Hananiah, of Shadrach; and to Mishael, of Meshach; and to Azariah, of Abednego.*
Daniel 1:6-7

- Hananiah — "The Lord is Gracious"
- Mishael — "Who is like God"
- Azariah — "The Lord helps"

Conquerors often stripped the previous culture of captives and installed a new one; to this end all three received new names. As teenagers in a foreign land, stripped of heritage and culture, how is it they maintained identity? By making up his mind long before taken captive, Daniel prepared himself for crisis, as once crisis arrives, it's a bit late to plot out a course of action.

> *But Daniel purposed in his heart that he would not defile himself with the portion of the king's food, nor with the wine which he drank; therefore he requested of the prince of the eunuchs that he might not defile himself.*  Daniel 1:8

It takes commitment and devotion to maintain in spite of circumstances. Daniel purposed in his heart — considerably before his deportation to Babylon. You must prepare *before* the situation arrives. Don't wait until it happens, that's too late. The same way a military soldier trains and prepares for any conceivable situation, consider how you'll respond *now*, before the situation arrives. You'd better prepare with Ephesians 6 as it's all the resources you're provided. Be sure you practice and train before you need it, and if areas of the armor require training and repair, begin training now.

A popular but incorrect idea says not to worry, as you'll rise to the occasion. Not so. You won't rise to the occasion, you'll respond as previously trained, and if no training exists to fall back on, well, a chicken running around comes to mind. Good luck.

The King's food wasn't kosher and had probably been offered to idols. Daniel (as a good Jew), would not want to violate kosher law, and requests only vegetables and water.

> *Now God had brought Daniel into favor and compassion with the prince of the eunuchs. And the prince of the eunuchs said unto Daniel, I fear my lord the king, who hath appointed your food and your drink; for why should he see your faces worse looking than the youths which are of your age? Then shall ye make me endanger my head to the king.*  Daniel 1:9–10

If Daniel and his friends health decline the penalty falls on Ashpenaz. To not follow the king's rules and have people in his care decline would endanger his life. Daniel was liked, but Ashpenaz could pay with his life as kings held absolute authority. Recall Esther as she called for three days of fasting before going into the King's chamber (Esther 4–5). You can't enter the presence of the king without being requested under penalty of death. Ashpenaz expresses valid concern — if Daniel's plan doesn't work, Ashpenaz is in big trouble.

### Chapter One

> *Then said Daniel to Melzar, whom the prince of the eunuchs had set over Daniel, Hananiah, Mishael, and Azariah, Test thy servants, I beseech thee, ten days; and let them give us vegetables to eat, and water to drink. Then let our countenances be looked upon before thee, and the countenance of the children that eat of the portion of the king's food; and as thou seest, deal with thy servants.*
> Daniel 1:11-13

A reasonable request by Daniel — try it and see if we're right. Notice Daniel accepted the scientific method.

1. Make a guess (we'll be fine with Kosher food).
2. Test it (wait 10 days).
3. Observe results (let our continuance be looked upon before you).

Daniel trusted the Lord to maintain his health while declining better food, but a big gamble for the guards. Why believe Daniel? Even the guards noticed differences between him and others. A quiet confidence and calm, because Daniel understood even at a young age who runs the show, and it's not Nebuchadnezzar.

> *So he consented to them in this matter, and tested them ten days. And at the end of ten days their countenances appeared fairer and fatter in flesh than all the youths which did eat the portion of the king's food.*
> Daniel 1:14-15

Even though they didn't eat food as good as others, God honors their commitment and sustains them. What resources exist won't matter to God. Too many pastors and churches judge success and if they're on the right course by two criteria: attendance and money.

Neither is correct. While the church requires resources to stay open, don't attribute any value to them as metrics or a clue to your standing with God. Rest assured, if God wants ministry "X" to continue, the status of the bank account holds no significance. Conversely, if a church wanders off track but holds a large bank account, they make a grave mistake equating it with God's blessing, or worse, God's approval.

> *Thus Melzar took away the portion of their food, and the wine that they should drink; and gave them vegetables. As for these four youths, God gave them knowledge and skill in all learning and wisdom; and Daniel had understanding in all visions and dreams.*
> Daniel 1:16-17

Who gave? God blessed them as a witness to a pagan king. Not based on receiving the best of what man can offer, but allowing the Lord to work. In chapter 2 we'll see God reveal to Daniel information all the king's magicians couldn't see.

> *Now at the end of the days that the king had said he should bring them in, then the prince of the eunuchs brought them in before Nebuchadnezzar. And the king conversed with them; and among them all was found none like Daniel, Hananiah, Mishael, and Azariah; therefore stood they before the king.*
> Daniel 1:18–19

Nebuchadnezzar sees them, and they're superior to the others. This causes jealousy and problems later as Daniel and his friends rise above other government officials, and those officials don't like it much. Politics hasn't changed in three thousand years.

> *And in all matters of wisdom and understanding, that the king inquired of them, he found them ten times better than all the magicians and astrologers that were in all his realm. And Daniel continued even unto the first year of king Cyrus.*
> Daniel 1:20–21

Daniel served in government for decades under several kings. No matter what the government, he rose to the top, a situation inconceivable today in a divided political environment where one administration brings in new people to replace the old, as they're from the "other" side. Daniel earned respect from multiple administrations, affirming his character and integrity.

*Chapter 3*

# Chapter Two

HAVE YOU EVER HAD A dream which bothered you? Perhaps a nightmare? Everyone dreams, and we're told we dream nightly if we don't remember. One night Nebuchadnezzar recognized the significance of his dream, disturbing him greatly.

> *And in the second year of the reign of Nebuchadnezzar, Nebuchadnezzar dreamed dreams wherewith his spirit was troubled, and his sleep went from him.*     Daniel 2:1

God commonly used dreams in the Old Testament era to communicate with people. However, it's not common today as we have the permanent indwelling of the Holy Spirit. When David prayed "take not thy Holy Spirit from me" he meant it — in the Old Testament the Spirit came and went (recall Samson and others); we easily forget our advantage over Old Testament people.

It's interesting God chose a Gentile to reveal the future of the world to; Nebuchadnezzar's dream shows all world empires until the end of time. Why didn't God reveal it to Daniel (as He did later in Chapter 7)? I don't know. Once again, God has His own reasons for His methods, and we don't always see or understand why. Using a Gentile was not without precedent in the Old Testament — recall Balaam (and his donkey) in Numbers 22; God uses anyone or anything He chooses to accomplish His goals.

> *Then the king commanded to summon the magicians, and the astrologers, and the sorcerers, and the Chaldeans, for to show the king his dreams. So they came and stood before the king. And the king said unto them, I have dreamed a dream, and my spirit was troubled to know the dream.*     Daniel 2:2–3

Before we examine the dream itself, it's useful to understand Nebuchadnezzar inherited these guys from his father. He hasn't worked with them much and in the back of his mind must wonder if they can do the job. He'll need advisers as he governs, but can they perform as they claim? Is their advice useful? The dream provides an opportunity to test them; most commentators believe the king knew the dream but had no idea what it meant — he's lying to test them. If he didn't recall the dream at all, how would he know if they provided the correct interpretation?

> *Then spoke the Chaldeans to the king in Aramaic, O king, live for ever; tell thy servants the dream, and we will show the interpretation.*
> Daniel 2:4

The interpretation can be faked given the content of the dream. But knowing the dream itself displayed your skill. The Chaldeans used books to explain dreams — symbols were looked up and the corresponding meanings. But how do you know it's right? That's Nebuchadnezzar's problem; anyone could make up the interpretation, how do you authenticate it?

Recall a story in Matthew 5 as people carry a paralytic man to Jesus. Instead of healing him, Jesus says "your sins are forgiven." Naturally, the scribes protest Jesus blasphemes, as who can forgive sins but God? Jesus responds by healing the man stating to the scribes so they may know He has power to forgive sins, He said rise and walk; the story validates Jesus' authority to forgive sins.

If someone says your sins are forgiven (and claims to be God), how do you authenticate it? By doing something only God could do. That's the point — by miraculous actions you validate the unconfirmable. That's what Nebuchadnezzar asks from his guys; validate your claims by actions ordinary people can't do. If you can, I'll *know* you provided the correct interpretation.

> *The king answered and said to the Chaldeans, the thing is gone from me. If ye will not make known unto me the dream, with the interpretation thereof, ye shall be cut in pieces, and your houses shall be made a refuse heap.*
> Daniel 2:5

Nebuchadnezzar needs to know if these guys possess the abilities they claim, so he provides a little motivation, with no further motivation required.

> *But if ye show the dream, and the interpretation thereof, ye shall receive of me gifts and rewards and great honor; therefore show me the dream, and the interpretation thereof.*   Daniel 2:6

High stakes in this game. It's feast or famine. Live or die. The carrot and the stick. If these guys possess the ability to perform, they have sufficient motivation to do it — it's Nebuchadnezzar's professional development program. He must determine if they're good or if he should fire them all.

> *They answered again and said, let the king tell his servants the dream, and we will show the interpretation of it.*
> Daniel 2:7

Nothing like this was ever asked before; they understood the impossibility of accomplishing what the king asked. In other words, they knew they were frauds (false teachers and prophets know they're frauds, but don't like to admit it).

> *The king answered and said, I know of certainty that ye would gain the time, because ye see the thing is gone from me. But if ye will not make known unto me the dream, there is but one decree for you; for ye have prepared lying and corrupt words to speak before me, till the time be changed; therefore tell me the dream, and I shall know that ye can show me the interpretation thereof.*   Daniel 2:8-9

If they can't reveal the dream, what other advice should the king follow from these guys? They're inept and untrustworthy; Nebuchadnezzar wants to verify these guys are worth the effort.

> *The Chaldeans answered before the king, and said, there is not a man upon the earth that can reveal the king's matter; therefore there is no king, lord, nor ruler, that asked such things at any magician, or astrologer, or Chaldean. And it is a rare thing that the king requireth, and there is none other that can reveal it before the king, except the gods, whose dwelling is not with flesh.*   Daniel 2:10-11

Truth comes from impostors. They know they're frauds, and what the king asks God alone can do. A true God can (and does) reveal unknown information and future events, separating the true God from others. Who can correctly declare future events? It's no problem for the true God, while a phony can't *always* be right. God Himself declares this as the differentiator.

> *Produce your cause, saith the LORD; bring forth your strong reasons, saith the King of Jacob. Let them bring them forth, and show us what shall happen; let them show the former things, what they be, that we may consider them, and know the latter end of them; or declare us things for to come. Show the things that are to come hereafter, that we may know that ye are gods; yea, do good, or do evil, that we may be dismayed, and behold it together. Behold, ye are of nothing, and your work of nought; an abomination is he that chooseth you.*
>
> Isaiah 41:21-24

So how do you know your god is God? That's a *very* important question. Many candidate gods exist, how do you choose one? Apply the test from Isaiah to candidates and see who predicts future events with certainty; God's Word proclaims events with accuracy — we've discussed Daniel's book contains accurate prophecy so critics must late-date it after the events took place (as critics deny the existence of god).

> *For this cause the king was angry and very furious, and commanded to destroy all the wise men of Babylon. And the decree went forth that the wise men should be slain; and they sought Daniel and his fellows to be slain.*
>
> Daniel 2:12-13

Daniel and his group are scheduled for execution with the impostors, as Nebuchadnezzar displays little tolerance for dissension. Once he makes a decision, that's it. He's disgusted with the performance of his advisers so decides to eliminate them and begin fresh with a new group. By his order they begin rounding up advisers, including Daniel.

> *Then Daniel answered with counsel and wisdom to Arioch the captain of the king's guard, which was gone forth to slay the wise men of Babylon. He answered and said to Arioch the king's captain, why is the decree so hasty from the king? Then Arioch made the thing known to Daniel.*
>
> Daniel 2:14-15

Daniel's wondering why all the chaos as Arioch informs Daniel of recent events, and instead of panicking Daniel has an idea. Did Daniel pray first, or believe and have confidence God would deliver him? We don't know, but I lean on the probability Daniel believed God would provide him the necessary knowledge.

# Chapter Two 21

> *Then Daniel went in, and desired of the king that he would give him time, and that he would show the king the interpretation.* Daniel 2:16

Daniel receives extra time the others didn't. Already Nebuchadnezzar notices differences between Daniel and the others. Maybe Nebuchadnezzar was skeptical, but wanted to know the dream's meaning, so allows Daniel a try.

God's people are always a little different. Your life (without broadcasting you're a Christian) should show people something different. If you're the same as everyone else, you've failed the course. As Chuck Missler says, if we ever arrive at the time when Christians are hauled into court, will enough evidence exist to convict you? Or are you an undercover Christian? Stealthy?

Christians running their own business bear an even higher fiduciary duty to act and live Godly lives. Many fail this duty; we wonder how many people reject Christianity due to the actions of Christians. Nobody should judge God by Christians — we're all imperfect and sinners by nature. A sad situation exists as many reject the salvation of Jesus Christ due to actions of misguided people calling themselves Christians.

> *Then Daniel went to his house, and made the thing known to Hananiah, Mishael, and Azariah, his companions; that they would desire mercies of the God of heaven concerning this secret; that Daniel and his fellows should not perish with the rest of the wise men of Babylon.* Daniel 2:17-18

Quite a prayer meeting. It's easy to lose focus during prayer, but facing these circumstances focus would not be a problem. Daniel enlists his friends; Daniel never tries to go it alone, grab credit for himself, or duck responsibility.

Daniel didn't know what would happen or if God would save them. Daniel trusted God, and knew no matter what happened, leaving the future to God proves the wisest strategy (his friends share the same characteristic as we'll discover in chapter 3). Trusting God is easy when events work themselves out, or you see the solution, but what if events don't go your way? That's when you find out if you trust the Lord.

Many people ask, why are some healed, and others not? Why do some suffer, and others not? I've learned the answer to the question is simply I don't know. I don't understand why events unfold as they do, and why some are spared and others not.

But instead of trying to understand earthly events, we need the divine viewpoint.

The classic example comes from Job, after almost everything he has disappeared in the first few chapters. The next thirty-five chapters his friends bloviate about why God might have done this — does he have sin or something else? And through thirty-five chapters no answer comes. The book of Job never answers what many consider the primary question — why the innocent suffer. It's not until late in the book the real lesson arrives from God (chapter 38:2–6, 40:8–9 and so on) as God intervenes and asks Job, where were you when I laid the foundation of the earth? In other words, I'm God, and you're not; Job finally obtains the divine viewpoint.

We don't always understand why things happen. It might appear the course is wrong, but as Bill Ritchie says "If God is God, then God is God." We need the divine viewpoint, and Job's conversation with God provides it. Don't look for understanding as it won't come; man can't provide reasons for why bad things happen.

> *Then was the secret revealed unto Daniel in a night vision. Then Daniel blessed the God of heaven. Daniel answered and said, blessed be the name of God for ever and ever; for wisdom and might are his, and he changeth the times and the seasons; he removeth kings, and setteth up kings; he giveth wisdom unto the wise, and knowledge to them that know understanding; He revealeth the deep and secret things; he knoweth what is in the darkness, and the light dwelleth with him. I thank thee, and praise thee, O thou God of my fathers, who hast given me wisdom and might, and hast made known unto me now what we desired of thee; for thou hast now made known unto us the king's matter.* Daniel 2:19–23

Daniel prays casually and simply. It's easy to sidetrack with many words, but God doesn't hear your many words or consider your actions, it's the attitude of your heart that counts. If you like to pray in thee's and thou's, fine. Just don't think God considers your prayer more because of your Olde English. It's the heart.

The Bible provides examples of brief prayers obtaining considerable results. Consider 1 Kings 18:21–38 as Elijah battles the prophets of Baal on Mount Carmel. Baal's prophets number four hundred and fifty, while Elijah stands alone (humanly speaking). The challenge is simple — each side builds an altar, calling on their god to send fire. Whichever god responds by fire, he is the true god.

The prophets of Baal spend most of the day calling on their god to no avail. Nobody listens or responds. When it's Elijah's turn, he prays briefly asking God to reveal He is the true God. And the fire of God fell consuming the altar, the sacrifice, and even the stones. It wasn't the many words or effort of Elijah prompting God to act, it's the attitude of the heart. The fervent prayer of a righteous man avails much (James 5:16).

> *Therefore Daniel went in unto Arioch, whom the king had ordained to destroy the wise men of Babylon; he went and said thus unto him; destroy not the wise men of Babylon. Bring me in before the king, and I will reveal unto the king the interpretation.* Daniel 2:24

It turns out Daniel saves the life of the phony magicians, but they don't exhibit much gratitude as later the people he saves plot to have him terminated. Politics hasn't changed much.

> *Then Arioch brought in Daniel before the king in haste, and said thus unto him, I have found a man of the captives of Judah, that will make known unto the king the interpretation.* Daniel 2:25

I have found? Did Arioch find Daniel? Contrast Arioch's attitude with Daniel's. Arioch attempts to take credit before the king for a minor role — finding someone to perform the king's request. Yet before the king Daniel refuses to take any glory for fulfilling the king's request.

> *The king answered and said to Daniel, whose name was Belteshazzar, art thou able to make known unto me the dream which I have seen, and the interpretation thereof?* Daniel 2:26

Here's a chance to build yourself up — are you the guy? It would be easy for Daniel to take credit as the king provides a perfect setup. Yet all through his life Daniel remains humble and gives glory to God.

> *Daniel answered in the presence of the king, and said, the secret which the king hath demanded cannot the wise men, the astrologers, the magicians, the soothsayers, reveal unto the king; but there is a God in heaven that revealeth secrets, and*

> *maketh known to the king Nebuchadnezzar what shall be in the latter days. Thy dream, and the visions of thy head upon thy bed, are these.*
> Daniel 2:27–28

Daniel doesn't draw attention to himself — he's transparent. He doesn't even say God revealed it as he woke up one morning. He simply states the existence of God, and He reveals secrets, and has spoken to the king concerning the latter days. Even with a setup from the king, Daniel refuses the opportunity to promote himself, as the disciple John reminds us "A man can receive nothing, except it be given him from heaven." The lesson is pride; don't take glory for yourself. If people notice you, you've failed.

> *As for thee, O king, thy thoughts came into thy mind upon thy bed, what should come to pass hereafter; and he that revealeth secrets maketh known to thee what shall come to pass. But as for me, this secret is not revealed to me for any wisdom that I have more than any living, but for their sakes that shall make known the interpretation to the king, and that thou mightest know the thoughts of thy heart.*
> Daniel 2:29–30

Daniel prefaces his comments by stating he's not special for this knowledge, but God provided it so the king will understand the dream. God could use anyone for this task; Daniel holds no special characteristics requiring God to use him over another. We all have talents and gifts from God; the possession of a skill or knowledge does not mean we're superior over others. Remember, God used Balam's donkey to proclaim His message.

> *Thou, O king, sawest, and behold a great image. This great image, whose brightness was excellent, stood before thee; and the form of it was terrible.*
> Daniel 2:31

Most commentators believe the image was mountain-sized and set behind a backdrop of mountains which may give the king the bad idea for the events in chapter 3 (Nebuchadnezzar frequently changed with whatever seemed good at the time). You need anchoring or you're open to deception and impression. Paul reminds us in Hebrews 2 to be firmly anchored or we're likely to drift away.

The antidote for deception and drifting follows from knowledge of your Bible; when deception comes you'll identify it. By studying truth you acquire the ability to detect a lie. Too many Christians lack this basic skill as they neglect the study of God's Word.

*This image's head was of fine gold, its breast and its arms of silver, its belly and its thighs of bronze, its legs of iron, its feet part of iron and part of clay.*    Daniel 2:32-33

The order of metals appears in decreasing specific gravity\* as well as monetary worth, as the following chart displays.

|              | Specific Gravity          | Value             |
|--------------|---------------------------|-------------------|
| Gold         | 19.3                      | $1,200/oz         |
| Silver       | 10.5                      | $20/oz            |
| Bronze       | 8.0                       | ?                 |
| Iron         | 7.5                       | ?                 |
| Iron + Clay  | < 5 (clay is about 2)     | dig it up outside |

*Thou sawest till that a stone was cut out without hands, which smote the image upon his feet that were of iron and clay, and broke them to pieces.*    Daniel 2:34

Acts 4:11, Ephesians 2:20, 1 Peter 2:4, and elsewhere describe the stone as Jesus Christ. First you should realize is who wins?

*Then was the iron, the clay, the bronze, the silver, and the gold, broken to pieces together, and became like the chaff of the summer threshing floors; and the wind carried them away, that no place was found for them; and the stone that smote the image became a great mountain, and filled the whole earth.*    Daniel 2:35

Not only defeated, but crushed. Isaiah 64:6 compares our righteousness to filthy rags; anything we offer to God is worthless, including our government. We may think we're good, but in God's view our works provide no value.

*This is the dream; and we will tell the interpretation thereof before the king.*    Daniel 2:36

Daniel doesn't pause to ask if he related the dream correctly — he knew he did as he maintained confidence in what God says. I wonder how many of us wouldn't pause a bit to see if we were right? Daniel had no doubts so moves directly to what the king wanted — the interpretation.

---

\*    Specific Gravity measures density compared to water. The higher the number, the more dense a substance is.

> *Thou, O king, art a king of kings; for the God of heaven hath given thee a kingdom, power, and strength, and glory. And wheresoever the children of men dwell, the beasts of the field and the fowls of the heaven hath he given into thine hand, and hath made thee ruler over them all. Thou art this head of gold.*
> Daniel 2:37-38

Jeremiah 27:6 specifically mentions God gave them all to Nebuchadnezzar. He didn't conquer from military skill, intelligence, or wealth. The basis for the king's success was God and Daniel makes this clear. Since the head of gold represents Nebuchadnezzar, he's the best — all others following will be inferior. Babylon ruled between 605–562 BC.*

> *And after thee shall arise another kingdom inferior to thee ...*
> Daniel 2:39a

Persia conquerors Babylon and rules from 539–330 BC. In Daniel 5:28–31 as Daniel interprets the handwriting on the wall for Belshazzar, he informs the king the Persians will conquer his kingdom. Of course, the prophecy is correct.

Persia was inferior in at least one way; not even the King could change a law once written. It's how Daniel finds himself in the lions' den, as in chapter 6 the King tries to save Daniel but is reminded he can't change the law. Contrast the Persians with Nebuchadnezzar who had ultimate authority and could do anything he wanted.

> *...and another third kingdom of bronze, which shall bear rule over all the earth.*
> Daniel 2:39b

Bronze represents Greece and Alexander the Great (332 BC). Daniel 11:1–4 predicts those events.

> *And the fourth kingdom shall be strong as iron, forasmuch as iron breaketh in pieces and subdueth all things; and as iron that breaketh all these, shall it break in pieces and bruise.*
> Daniel 2:40

---

\*   We're going to skip historic details and use approximate dates. Anyone wishing to obtain historic details the answers are as close as the library. For our purposes the history of who conquered who and how is irrelevant.

Iron represents Rome who conquered in 70 BC. But who conquers Rome? Nobody, it fell apart from corruption. While noted for brutality, Rome maintained law and order, and in the end collapsed from internal corruption.

> *And whereas thou sawest the feet and toes, part of potters' clay, and part of iron, the kingdom shall be divided; but there shall be in it of the strength of the iron, forasmuch as thou sawest the iron mixed with miry clay.* Daniel 2:41

This is *not* a fifth kingdom, it's the fourth (Rome) rebuilt in a separate phase which yet future. How do we know? Daniel himself doesn't identify it as a fifth kingdom in chapter 3; in Daniel 7 we see the same sequence but as God sees it (nasty beasts compared to shiny valuable metals). Many Bibles cross-reference the verses in chapter 7 back to chapter 2.

> *In the first year of Belshazzar king of Babylon Daniel had a dream and visions of his head upon his bed; then he wrote the dream, and told the sum of the matters. Daniel spoke and said, I saw in my vision by night, and, behold, the four winds of the heaven strove upon the great sea. And four great beasts came up from the sea, diverse one from another. The first was like a lion, and had eagle's wings; I beheld till the wings thereof were plucked, and it was lifted up from the earth, and made stand upon the feet as a man, and a man's heart was given to it. And behold another beast, a second, like to a bear, and it raised up itself on one side, and it had three ribs in the mouth of it between the teeth of it; and they said thus unto it, arise, devour much flesh. After this I beheld, and lo another, like a leopard, which had upon the back of it four wings of a fowl; the beast had also four heads; and dominion was given to it. After this I saw in the night visions, and behold a fourth beast, dreadful and terrible, and strong exceedingly; and it had great iron teeth; it devoured and broke in pieces, and stamped the residue with the feet of it; and it was diverse from all the beasts that were before it; and it had ten horns. I considered the horns, and, behold, there came up among them another little horn, before whom there were three of the first horns plucked up by the roots; and, behold, in this horn were eyes like the eyes of man, and a mouth speaking great things.* Daniel 7:1–8

Only four beasts appear in chapter 7; the same events display from two different frames of reference — man's and God's. From man's view it appears five kingdoms exist since thousands of years passed and the rebuilt Roman empire hasn't yet appeared. But since God exists outside time He doesn't see the difference between the two phases of the Roman empire.

Since then, many tried for world dominion and failed. Spain, England, Germany (twice), etc. All failed. But a revived Roman empire will reappear.

> *And as the toes of the feet were part of iron, and part of clay, so the kingdom shall be partly strong, and partly broken. And whereas thou sawest iron mixed with miry clay, they shall mingle themselves with the seed of men; but they shall not adhere one to another, even as iron is not mixed with clay.*
> Daniel 2:42–43

Clay generally represents people, so the second phase holds together by people, or treaty. It will not be a single entity, but a conglomeration of nations and will not be stable (compare chapter 7 with chapter 2). One guy comes forward and pulls it together. Known as the Antichrist, but better known as the coming world leader. What are his characteristics?*

- Intellectual genius: Daniel 7:20, 8:23, Ezekiel 28:3
- Persuasive orator: Daniel 7:20, Revelation 13:2
- Shrewd political manipulator: Daniel 11:21
- Successful commercial genius: Daniel 8:25, Revelation 13:17, Psalm 52:7, Daniel 11:38, 43, Ezekiel 28:4–5
- Forceful military leader: Daniel 8:24, Revelation 6:2, Revelation 13:4
- Powerful organizer: Revelation 13:1–2, 17:17
- Unifying religious guru: 2 Thessalonians 2:4, Revelation 13:3,14,15

He holds many titles through the Bible: Antichrist, man of sin, lawless one, prince of darkness, son of perdition, prince that shall come, idol shepherd, and so on. Antichrist remains the popular title, but the Bible generally doesn't speak of him that way. If you're focused on the Antichrist, you'll miss many references. Consider a few characteristics about this guy the Bible does reveal.

> *Let no man deceive you by any means; for that day shall not come, except there come the falling away first, and that man of*

---

\* Missler (1991, page 10)

> *sin be revealed, the son of perdition, who opposeth and exalteth himself above all that is called God, or that is worshiped; so that he as God sitteth in the temple of God, showing himself that he is God.* 2 Thessalonians 2:3–4

Two of his titles appear in this letter, so we know who Paul speaks of. Paul includes a note this guy will appear in the temple and demand worship as God. This act holds a specific title — the abomination of desolation. In Matthew 24 Jesus speaks of the same event, and in a comment in the text you are admonished to understand. Many fear prophecy and end times, yet you are called to understand. Why? So you won't be deceived.

Paul says let no one deceive you; a time will come when you will be openly lied to (many would say that time is now, but it will get worse). If you're young you've grown up with deception and corruption — even in our nation's highest office. It used to be a handshake could seal even large and complex deals without legions of lawyers, but those times went extinct like dinosaurs.

One example of deception comes from the political world — "budget cuts." When a politician speaks of budget cuts, it doesn't mean what normal people think of. Most would think if you had $100, and you were cut monetarily, you end up with less than $100. But in the alternative reality politicians live in, if a budget one year receives $100 million, and next year they receive $120 million, but asked for $130 million, that's a "cut" of $10 million (not an increase of $20 million). Absurd, isn't it? But don't believe it; watch the news and you'll notice this sleight of hand all the time. The fantasy land of politics provides an example of Orwellian doublethink, defined in the book "1984."

> *The power of holding two contradictory beliefs in one's mind simultaneously, and accepting both of them. ... To tell deliberate lies while genuinely believing in them, to forget any fact that has become inconvenient, and then, when it becomes necessary again, to draw it back from oblivion for just so long as it is needed, to deny the existence of objective reality and all the while to take account of the reality which one denies all this is indispensably necessary. Even in using the word doublethink it is necessary to exercise doublethink. For by using the word one admits that one is tampering with reality; by a fresh act of doublethink one erases this knowledge; and so on indefinitely, with the lie always one leap ahead of the truth.\**

---

\*   Orwell (1949, page 176–177)

As deception increases the only antidote comes from your knowledge of God's Word (not God's Word itself, but how skilled you are wielding it). As a believer in the inerrant Word of God you will be unpopular and non politically correct. In fact, most of the church will buy into deception — all those churches not needing new pastors after the rapture.

That's not being harsh, it's a fact. Jesus said not all in the church are true when He related the parable of the wheat and tares in Matthew 13:24–30. Many people misunderstand the parables in Matthew 13; they don't mean the church will take over the world, but the church will be impure. In this parable, we don't need to guess the meaning as Jesus Himself delivers the interpretation in verses 36–43. The tares (which grow with the wheat) represent workers of Satan!

Specific deceptions appear in the tribulation *after* the rapture (so we won't see them), but don't make the mistake life continues on its easy course until then. Not so, deception increases daily. The pre-trib position can cause people to believe before it gets tough we're out of here. Not necessarily so. Persecution followed most of the church for most of history, while the United States escaped it; no guarantee exists it will last.

*And then shall that wicked be revealed, whom the Lord shall consume with the spirit of his mouth, and shall destroy with the brightness of his coming, even him, whose coming is after the working of Satan with all power and signs and lying wonders.* 2 Thessalonians 2:8–9

Satan himself pours all his resources into this guy, and he doesn't make it. Another misconception (even among Christians), concerns the awaiting epic battle between Satan and God. A final conflict will occur, but it's not much of a battle. Consider also what John says in Revelation 13:1–5.

*And I stood upon the sand of the sea, and saw a beast rise up out of the sea, having seven heads and ten horns, and upon his horns ten crowns, and upon his heads the name of blasphemy. And the beast which I saw was like unto a leopard, and his feet were as the feet of a bear, and his mouth as the mouth of a lion; and the dragon gave him his power, and his throne, and great authority. And I saw one of his heads as it were wounded to death; and his deadly wound was healed, and all the world wondered after the beast. And they worshiped the dragon which gave power unto the beast; and they worshiped the beast, saying, who is like unto the beast? Who is able to make war with him? And there was given unto him a mouth speaking great things and blasphemies; and power was given unto him to continue forty and two months.* Revelation 13:1–5

Does that sound familiar? Leopard, bear, lion? Daniel 7? Revelation 13 ties in with this vision in chapter 2. Notice the consistency of idioms and how all tie together throughout the Bible. Chuck Missler says the Bible is an integrated message system — even though forty authors wrote over thousands of years.

This disproves another skeptic argument on the Bible. If you've heard the skeptic sneer "you're using the Bible to prove itself, that's circular reasoning and a logical error" you can use these passages (and others) to prove not only how pathetic their "logic" is, but how they don't know what they're talking about concerning the Bible.

Circular reasoning (or using what you're trying to prove as an argument of proof) should be avoided, *assuming you're using one book or author.* But the Bible exists as a compilation of many individual books and authors written over thousands of years — even the most jaded skeptic will admit it.

Thus, when John authenticates Daniel, or John cites Isaiah, or any of the dozens of authors cites another written hundreds of years apart, it *can't* be circular reasoning, as the Bible lives as sixty-six books written by forty guys hundreds or thousands of years apart. The skeptic looks foolish and ignorant attempting the circular reasoning argument; it shows they haven't studied the book they claim to be a critic on.

... and another skeptic argument on the Bible bites the dust.

42 months equals 3 ½ years, another clue to the length of time of the great tribulation. Bible prophecy uses 360 day years, so a period of 3 ½ years can be given several ways.

- 42 months — Revelation 11:2, 13:5
- 1,260 days — Revelation 11:3, 12:6
- Half of one week (literally "sevens") — Daniel 9:27
- Times, time and half a time — Daniel 12:7

With a brief introduction to deception and the Antichrist, we'll return to Daniel.

*And in the days of these kings shall the God of heaven set up a kingdom, which shall never be destroyed; and the kingdom*

> *shall not be left to other people, but it shall break in pieces and consume all these kingdoms, and it shall stand for ever.*
>
> Daniel 2:44

Revelation 19:11–16 fills in details Daniel doesn't provide, a reminder the Bible remains its own best commentary.

> *And I saw heaven opened, and behold a white horse; and he that sat upon him was called Faithful and True, and in righteousness he doth judge and make war. His eyes were as a flame of fire, and on his head were many crowns; and he had a name written, that no man knew, but he himself. And he was clothed with a vesture dipped in blood; and his name is called The Word of God. And the armies which were in heaven followed him upon white horses, clothed in fine linen, white and clean. And out of his mouth goeth a sharp sword, that with it he should smite the nations, and he shall rule them with a rod of iron; and he treadeth the winepress of the fierceness and wrath of Almighty God. And he hath on his vesture and on his thigh a name written, KING OF KINGS, AND LORD OF LORDS.*
>
> Revelation 19:11–16

Daniel concludes by telling the king God provided him knowledge of what will come, and the certainty of the interpretation.

> *Forasmuch as thou sawest that the stone was cut out of the mountain without hands, and that it broke in pieces the iron, the bronze, the clay, the silver, and the gold; the great God hath made known to the king what shall come to pass hereafter; and the dream is certain, and the interpretation of it sure.*
>
> Daniel 2:45

It's revealed to us as well as Daniel ties in with other prophecy. By studying the Bible as a complete and integrated message, you'll notice other passages illuminate and expand on others. One big mistake made in Bible study occurs from not allowing the Bible to comment on itself. In Daniel chapter 2, notice how many details appear elsewhere in the Bible.

> *Then the king Nebuchadnezzar fell upon his face, and worshiped Daniel, and commanded that they should offer an oblation and sweet odors unto him.*
>
> Daniel 2:46

Nebuchadnezzar gives glory to Daniel instead of God. As already seen, Nebuchadnezzar can be easily swayed by whatever appears before him; he lacks a foundation in anything.

> *The king answered unto Daniel, and said, of a truth it is, that your God is the God of gods, and a Lord of kings, and a revealer of secrets, seeing thou couldest reveal this secret.*
> Daniel 2:47

Nebuchadnezzar is a little fickle — he follows anything appearing good at the time. Here he's right, but in chapter 3 he wanders off track.

> *Then the king made Daniel a great man, and gave him many great gifts, and made him ruler over the whole province of Babylon, and chief of the governors over all the wise men of Babylon. Then Daniel requested of the king, and he set Shadrach, Meshach, and Abednego, over the affairs of the province of Babylon; but Daniel sat in the gate of the king.*
> Daniel 2:48–49

Daniel rises to the top of the government. Not only under Nebuchadnezzar, but later in the Persian empire as well.

*Chapter 4*

# Chapter Three

THESE EVENTS TAKE PLACE roughly ten years following chapter 2; scholars debate exact timeframes (ranging from 2–30 years), but the events don't immediately follow chapter 2; time passed allowing all parties to dwell on previous events and plot revenge. At the end of chapter 2 the Jewish captives rose to power in Babylon; the rest of the Chaldeans resented them, waiting for their opportunity for revenge. Now is the time.

> *Nebuchadnezzar the king made an image of gold, whose height was threescore cubits, and the breadth thereof six cubits: he set it up in the plain of Dura, in the province of Babylon.*
> Daniel 3:1

Politics hasn't changed much. It's popular to say "every day in every way we're getting better and better," but it's not true. The idea's popularity (the reversing of entropy or returning to order from chaos) stems from its requirement for evolution (a fairy tale for another time); comparing politics thousands of years ago in Daniel to recent elections doesn't yield much difference. Politics is (and always has been) a dirty and nasty business — it's not for the faint of heart.

Nebuchadnezzar creates a colossal image from gold; recall the previous chapter when Nebuchadnezzar sees the image — it had a chest of silver, stomach of bronze, and so on. By building his image entirely of gold, is this Nebuchadnezzar claiming immortality?

Man continuously seeks the fountain of youth or immortality. From strange religions to various pills, creams, and potions, everything man does strives to extend his life, denying the fact that from your birth your body begins rotting, and nothing you do can stop it (ironically we are all immortal, the only question is where you will spend it).

> *Then Nebuchadnezzar the king sent to gather together the princes, the governors, and the captains, the judges, the treasurers, the counselors, the sheriffs, and all the rulers of the provinces, to come to the dedication of the image which Nebuchadnezzar the king had set up.*
> Daniel 3:2

Long-winded way to say, everybody.

> *Then the princes, the governors, and captains, the judges, the treasurers, the counselors, the sheriffs, and all the rulers of the provinces, were gathered together unto the dedication of the image that Nebuchadnezzar the king had set up; and they stood before the image that Nebuchadnezzar had set up.*
> Daniel 3:3

Everyone bowed (pun intended) to political correctness and followed the herd. Exodus 23:2 warns concerning the dangers of following a crowd — don't do it. You must be wary of the herd mentality; just because everyone does it doesn't make it acceptable. Great tragedies occur because "everyone else does it." God gave you a brain and the capacity to reason — use it.

> *"What defines your morality?" I asked with genuine curiosity.*
>
> *There was an extended pause as Dawkins considered the question carefully. "Moral philosophic reasoning and a shifting zeitgeist." ...*
>
> *I asked an obvious question: "As we speak of this shifting zeitgeist, how are we to determine who's right? ...*
>
> *"Yes, absolutely fascinating." His response was immediate. "What's to prevent us from saying Hitler wasn't right? I mean, that is a genuinely difficult question. But whatever [defines morality], it's not the Bible. If it was, we'd be stoning people for breaking the Sabbath."*
>
> *I was stupefied. He had readily conceded that his own philosophical position did not offer a rational basis for moral judgments. His intellectual honesty was refreshing, if somewhat disturbing on this point.\**

---

\*    Taunton (2007)

# Chapter Three

In the 1940s, everything Hitler heaped on the Jews and others was popular and legal, but popularity and legality can't justify it. Executing millions of people remains since time began a staggering exhibition of evil, and a majority of people failing to stop Hitler's insane ideas doesn't make them right. A scary idea in politics is "majority rules." Yes, that should be true for taxes and bureaucratic rules, but right and wrong won't be found by surveys; the majority view can lead to tyranny. As a Christian, don't follow the crowd. In this case, these three guys recognized the error and took a stand against it.

> *Then an herald cried aloud, to you it is commanded, O people, nations, and languages, that at the time ye hear the sound of the horn, pipe, lyre, sackbut, psaltery, dulcimer, and all kinds of music, ye fall down and worship the golden image that Nebuchadnezzar the king hath set up; and whoso falleth not down and worshippeth shall the same hour be cast into the midst of a burning fiery furnace.* Daniel 3:4–6

Local pagans in Babylon worshiped multiple gods, so a decree of this sort would not be a problem for the general population — the decree only bothers monotheistic Jews. The locals worshiped anything and everything; adding one more god could be beneficial. After all, what if this missed god we need for help with finances or crops?

> *Therefore at that time, when all the people heard the sound of the horn, pipe, lyre, sackbut, psaltery, and all kinds of music, all the people, the nations, and the languages, fell down and worshiped the golden image that Nebuchadnezzar the king had set up.* Daniel 3:7

The politically correct herd does what the herd always does — do what everyone else does. Yet conforming to a set of rules isn't limited to the politically correct crowd. Even non-conformists follow the rule; from the sixties flower children to anarchists of today, the non-conformist crowd *always* conforms to their own set of rules, punishing anyone who doesn't follow. In other words, you must non-conform as everyone else (in a conforming manner).

Conforming to a group grows so strong Matthew Henry said "there is nothing so bad which the careless world will not be drawn to by a concert of music, or driven to by a fiery furnace." Or as Satan said in Job 2 "Skin for skin. Yes, all that a man has will he give for his life." Man maintains a strong desire for self-preservation, and going against the grain for these guys must have been distressing. Someone once said "A hero isn't braver than any other man, he's just braver longer."

> *Wherefore at that time certain Chaldeans came near, and accused the Jews.*
> Daniel 3:8

These guys were likely the ones showed up from chapter 2, but they exhibit a strange sense of gratitude. Again, politics hasn't changed much. Even though Daniel spared their lives by interpreting the dream, they seethe with resentment and anger, waiting years for their chance at revenge, and won't allow an opportunity to float by.

All through history Jews suffer attacks. As God clarified His plan for the Messiah to appear, it provided Satan more information to focus his attacks. The Jews have been threatened with extinction because if they don't exist, a Jewish Messiah can't appear and mans' hope of redemption vanishes.

> *They spoke and said to the king Nebuchadnezzar, O king, live for ever. Thou, O king, hast made a decree, that every man that shall hear the sound of the horn, pipe, lyre, sackbut, psaltery, and dulcimer, and all kinds of music, shall fall down and worship the golden image; And whoso falleth not down and worshippeth, that he should be cast into the midst of a burning fiery furnace. There are certain Jews whom thou hast set over the affairs of the province of Babylon, Shadrach, Meshach, and Abednego; these men, O king, have not regarded thee; they serve not thy gods, nor worship the golden image which thou hast set up.*
> Daniel 3:9–12

Politics hasn't changed in thousands of years. It remains a nasty cut-throat business, with people possessing long memories. Likely Daniel's adversaries still resent the events of the previous chapter, spending years waiting for a suitable opportunity to launch an attack on his friends. With the absence of Daniel, they seize their opportunity.

> *Then Nebuchadnezzar in his rage and fury commanded to bring Shadrach, Meshach, and Abednego. Then they brought these men before the king. Nebuchadnezzar spoke and said unto them, Is it true, O Shadrach, Meshach, and Abednego, do not ye serve my gods, nor worship the golden image which I have set up? Now if ye be ready that at what time ye hear the*

## Chapter Three

*sound of the horn, pipe, lyre, sackbut, psaltery, and dulcimer, and all kinds of music, ye fall down and worship the image which I have made; well; but if ye worship not, ye shall be cast the same hour into the midst of a burning fiery furnace; and who is that God that shall deliver you out of my hands?*
Daniel 3:13-15

Nebuchadnezzar was rash, impulsive, and impressionable — you didn't cross him. Unlike the President, the King held complete authority; he could do anything he wanted. He retained the power over life and death — he could change laws anytime he desired.

Nebuchadnezzar decides to provide another chance as perhaps they didn't hear the music, or became confused. His decree required execution as soon as they failed to bow down, so he's bending the rules a little for them. Nebuchadnezzar exercised flexibility enforcing the law, but later empires didn't grant that ability to the king (laws of the Persians could not be changed, see chapter 6).

*Shadrach, Meshach, and Abednego, answered and said to the king, O Nebuchadnezzar, we are not careful to answer thee in this matter.*
Daniel 3:16

They violate a certain protocol addressing the king. Certain presidents have been less than stellar, yet if I met them I would address them as Mr. President. It's basic protocol and respect (for the office, if not the man). These three Hebrews inform the king where to put his absurd law, refusing to disobey God (Thou shalt have no other gods before me Exodus 20:3).

Incivility in politics hasn't changed much either. Newt Gingrich stated all candidates should be required to meet and travel together for a few reasons. First, it would be good for the country to hear multiple points of view at once. Too many times a candidate never ventures outside his own base and isn't exposed to opposing views. Second, it's much harder to be vile and mean when a person stands right next to you; if you can do that it means you lack civility and shouldn't be in public office anyway.

These Hebrews don't hesitate while facing an uncertain outcome. It's easy for us to recline and ponder the story, but this must have been an intimidating moment before the king; their conviction and courage stands firm.

As Nebuchadnezzar queries "What god is able to deliver you?" to these men we need an answer as well. Not God being all-powerful, but a response demonstrating the superiority of God's plan in all situations. We attempt to defend God and don't need to. God can defend Himself; only simple statements of facts are required, as our boys demonstrate. Romans 13 states Christians should follow government law *unless* it violates God's law.

> *Let every soul be subject unto the higher powers. For there is no power but of God; the powers that be are ordained of God. Whosoever therefore resisteth the power, resisteth the ordinance of God; and they that resist shall receive to themselves judgment. Wherefore ye must needs be subject, not only for wrath, but also for conscience sake.* Romans 13:1—2,5

Or clearer in the NLT:

> *Everyone must submit to governing authorities. For all authority comes from God, and those in positions of authority have been placed there by God. So anyone who rebels against authority is rebelling against what God has instituted, and they will be punished. So you must submit to them, not only to avoid punishment, but also to keep a clear conscience.*

That's pretty clear, isn't it? If you know any Roman Empire history and how they treated the early church, it's a bold statement from Paul. Paul says obey governing authorities without listing an exception for laws or rules you don't like. At the dawn of the pandemic age (2019—2021) the church and its pastors became mired in political quagmire, as a popular new doctrine swept across the American church of "we don't have to follow laws we don't like" (during a pandemic or otherwise) in direct contradiction to Paul.

Arguing (or replacing) Paul's teaching isn't a good idea, in the first century or today as pastors promote strange new doctrine of rebellion and lawlessness, casting off Paul's words simply because they don't like them.

Wait a minute you say, doesn't an exception exist? Sort of.

> *Then Peter and the other apostles answered and said, We ought to obey God rather than men.* Acts 5:29

What was the situation in Acts 5? The disciples were told not to preach in Jesus' name — an order they can't follow. You don't get a blank check to ignore laws you don't like. Let's be honest, all of us view some actions the government performs as wrong and we'd like to change (or ignore), but in light of Paul's teaching, is that correct? Or woefully out of order?

The dawn of the pandemic age revealed a not insignificant group of pastors willfully and proudly abandoning the Bible as God's Word to be followed (the fact they're *proud* of their actions is also revealing). Those pastors cause a large group of Christians to follow them off the road into a ditch as their new doctrine promotes political action, rebellion, and politics over ministry.

Keep in mind *the* fruit of the spirit: love. If a pastor creates division and strife, demonstrating hostility towards others not sharing his political beliefs while quarreling and arguing over non-doctrinal personal opinions, do his actions align with the fruit of the spirit, or the fruit of the flesh (Galatians 5:19)?

Only one exception exists, and it's narrow and (at least in the United States) *extremely* rare. We don't need to guess on application, as examples in Daniel prove correct application. *One* exception exists with Paul's instruction demonstrated in Daniel: if we are told to oppose Christ (i.e. bow down to idols, deny Christ, etc.), as is the case with Daniel's three buddies. But that's it, and it's a narrow exception.

> *If it be so, our God whom we serve is able to deliver us from the burning fiery furnace, and he will deliver us out of thine hand, O king. But if not, be it known unto thee, O king, that we will not serve thy gods, nor worship the golden image which thou hast set up.* Daniel 3:17-18

These guys don't lack chutzpah, or we can call it dedication. They didn't know if they would live or not, but their dedication never wavered. They understood a foundational principle — God would deliver from death or through death, and it didn't matter which. No matter what happened, God delivers from Nebuchadnezzar.

Reread Daniel chapter 1 as he purposed in his heart not to yield to the society he lived in. You must make the commitment *before* the situation presents itself; once you're standing before the king it's too late to make your mind up. Decide on your commitment now. If you have areas needing shoring up, do it. If you need practice with the armor of God, work on it. You have time now; later you might not.

At points life stinks, and might stink a lot for a long time. Not a popular idea though, but it's true; Jesus guaranteed trials would come (John 16:33). He stated the rain falls on the bad and the good (Matthew 5:45). People debate if the rain is bad or good, but the debate misses the point. Whether it's good or bad it falls on everyone. You will have tough times. You can pout and whine, or face them head-on. Your choice.

Many people ask why do we have trials? Why do bad things happen to good people? Recall Genesis 22 as God told Abraham to offer Isaac. At the last moment an angel stopped Abraham (God doesn't advocate child sacrifice). Why was this played out? Did God need to know Abraham's character? Of course not. But *Abraham* needed to know his character. Like Abraham God wants you to know, did I yield or stay committed? How did I handle that situation? What areas am I doing good in, and what areas need help?

Second, bad things happen to everyone, and frequently the only people understanding are those who've crawled over the same ground. You have the opportunity to help others in similar problems in a way people who haven't experienced them can't. Experiencing difficulties yields a unique perspective, one you can't obtain any other way — it's important to share that knowledge.

> *Blessed be God, even the Father of our Lord Jesus Christ, the Father of mercies, and the God of all comfort; Who comforteth us in all our tribulation, that we may be able to comfort them which are in any trouble, by the comfort wherewith we ourselves are comforted of God.*   2 Corinthians 1:3-4

One of Satan's strategies attempts to make you believe you're all alone. Imagine these three guys — thousands bow down and they're all alone. It's basic human nature to desire to fit in with the crowd and do what everyone else does. Even during the '60s when the motto was non-conformance, everyone non-conformed to the same standard. But these guys never forgot they never were alone.

> *But now thus saith the LORD that created thee, O Jacob, and he that formed thee, O Israel, fear not; for I have redeemed thee, I have called thee by thy name; thou art mine. When thou passest through the waters, I will be with thee; and through the rivers, they shall not overflow thee; when thou walkest through the fire, thou shalt not be burned; neither shall the flame kindle upon thee.*   Isaiah 43:1-2

When you go through fiery trials — it's going to happen. Remember God hasn't forgotten you and promises to carry you through, but maybe not like you'd imagine (or want). When God says let's go to the other side of the lake He doesn't detail how, but you will arrive on the other side. These guys had no promise of any particular outcome, but refused to yield.

Yet some erroneously say if God will deliver me, I'll sit and wait for the Lord to act. You must not say "God will provide" and do nothing. People refuse doctors believing if God will cure me, there's no reason to go to the doctor. Proverbs 21:31 states the horse is prepared for the day of battle; but safety is of the LORD. In other words, you must do everything you can to prepare, avoiding two common mistakes:

- Not preparing — If you need a job, start looking. If sick, go to a doctor. If a hurricane is arriving, do what you can to prepare and take precautions for safety.
- Being prepared, but trusting in your preparations. After doing all the prep work, your safety isn't in what you've done, it's from God. Ultimately it's not the surgeon, or the oncologist, or the radiologist, or the cardiologist, or the cosmologist providing the cure (OK the last one is a joke).

The simple lesson from Daniel 3 — our God can deliver, and even if He doesn't don't bow down to fear or man or anything else. We will do what we can to prepare but then trust in the Lord; even if events don't end the way we wish, God's plan proves superior to anything we can think of.

So how do we prepare for trials coming our way?

First, be prepared. Daniel purposed in his heart not to defile himself back in chapter 1. Decide now how you'll respond. When events overcome you, it's too late to derive a course of action. You need to decide how you'll respond now. Don't wait.

Second, you must be stubborn. Stubbornness can be good (chapter 3), but also bad (chapter 4). Don't make the mistake it's always bad to exhibit stubbornness and a single will, as Winston Churchill illustrates.

*We shall go on to the end, we shall fight in France, we shall fight on the seas and oceans, we shall fight with growing confidence and growing strength in the air, we shall defend our Island, whatever the cost may be, we shall fight on the beaches, we shall fight on the landing grounds, we shall fight in the fields and in the streets, we shall fight in the hills; we shall never surrender...*

Paul reminds us in Hebrews 2:1 to give earnest heed to the things we have heard, lest at any time we should let them slip; if you're not ready and prepared drifting becomes certain. Paul speaks in nautical terms in Hebrews; you must anchor to something stronger than yourself. As a ship anchors, it's an obvious requirement to anchor to something stronger than the ship itself. We are no different from the ship; too many people attempt to anchor to money, or possessions, or education; none of those provide the strength required. Only anchoring to the Lord provides the stability you need.

Once anchored, you can react like these guys because no choice exists. You're going to do what you can (prepare the horse for battle), but know deliverance comes from God (safety is of the Lord). No matter what happens you can be confident in the best result. Consider a few examples.

- Job 13:15 — Job says though he slay me, yet will I trust Him. We know what Job went through (read chapters 1–2) as he lost almost everything — family, possessions, livestock. All he had was his wife, whose great advice was curse God and die. Yet through it all Job maintained his trust in God.
- Acts 4 — Peter before the Sanhedrin when he's told to no longer speak about Jesus. In verses 19–20 Peter states we cannot but speak the things we have seen. In short, take a hike.
- Acts 5 — After being thrown in prison and ordered not to teach in Jesus' name, they do anyway and Peter says we ought to obey God rather than men. We will not bow down.
- Acts 7 — Stephen's address before the Sanhedrin. His bold move only inflames them and ultimately moves them to stone Stephen. Yet Stephen maintained and refused to yield, which likely would have spared his life.

But that's tough to do all the time as many times we feel like the disciples in Mark 4:35–40 as they encountered problems crossing the lake.

*And the same day, when the evening was come, he saith unto them, Let us pass over unto the other side. And when they had sent away the multitude, they took him even as he was in the boat. And there were also with him other little boats. And there arose a great storm of wind, and the waves beat into the boat, so that it was now full. And he was in the stern part of the ship, asleep on a pillow; and they awake him, and say unto him, Master, carest thou not that we perish?* Mark 4:35–38

Feel like that? While the ship sinks, the Lord sleeps. Don't you care? Aren't you going to do something? The disciples travel with the creator of the universe yet display incredible fear. Perhaps Shadrach, Meshach and Abed-Nego thought where is God? Why isn't He acting? Why has He abandoned us? Notice what occurred when the disciples displayed their lack of faith.

*And he arose, and rebuked the wind, and said unto the sea, Peace, be still. And the wind ceased, and there was a great calm. And he said unto them, Why are ye so fearful? How is it that ye have no faith?* Mark 4:39–40

Many believe the disciples lacked faith in His deity. Yet that doesn't make sense when they woke Jesus up; on some level they understood Jesus had the power to help them. The faith they lacked was in His promise to arrive at the other side. They knew Jesus was God, but lacked faith in His promise to execute His plan.

God doesn't guarantee an easy ride, and that's when problems creep in. Don't read into promises of God ideas not contained therein. In Mark 4 Jesus says we're going to the other side, but didn't make any statement regarding the conditions of the journey. The disciples surmised when the storm came up it voided the promise of Jesus. Not so.

But this was no natural storm. These professional fishermen spent their lives on this body of water; their terror meant this storm was particularly brutal. No matter the storm, how much effort did Jesus expend to eliminate it? Two words.

Were they ever in danger? No. Did they act like it? No. And that's the problem. We possess the same advantage they did as the creator of the universe travels along with us as well. And we forget it as easily as they did. Somewhere in there hides a lesson we should learn.

This doesn't mean you'll always be cured, or delivered from the fiery furnace. Only God's plan is the best and it's guaranteed. But our human survival isn't. The prosperity doctrine God wants you to be cured, have a big house with a large bank account, a Lexus (and a pony and ice cream), and if you don't it's because you lack faith isn't true, considering Paul and his thorn in the flesh. Three times he prayed for its removal, yet wasn't delivered. God said his grace was sufficient — healing isn't coming. And Paul's conclusion?

> *Most gladly therefore will I rather glory in my infirmities, that the power of Christ may rest upon me. Therefore I take pleasure in infirmities, in reproaches, in necessities, in persecutions, in distresses for Christ's sake: for when I am weak, then am I strong.*   2 Corinthians 12:9-10

I doubt Paul lacked faith, the reason he wasn't healed hasn't been revealed. We don't know why, and perhaps Paul never learned why either. But he did learn God has a reason, and it's better to trust Him. It's a simple axiom desperate times create more intense and passionate prayer. And the more desperate the situation, the more we trust ourselves less, and Him more. That's the point.

Sometimes life appears desperate — to us. My God is able to deliver, and even if He doesn't I won't bow down to fear, or man's wisdom, or false doctrines of prosperity. If God is God, then God is God (Bill Ritchie).

In 2 Kings 6 as the Syrian army surrounds Elisha he doesn't act bothered by it. His servant expresses considerable unrest, waking up Elisha. Elisha responds cryptically "they that are with us are more than they that are with them," increasing the servant's confusion. Elisha realizes he won't sleep much unless he deals with this problem, so he asks the Lord to let him in on the secret and the servant sees horses and chariots of fire all around Elisha. God hadn't forgotten them (Elisha knew it, the servant didn't), and He won't forget you either.

In the next chapter (2 Kings 7) during a Syrian siege of the city the situation becomes desperate. Elisha appears on the scene and says don't worry, by tomorrow this will be gone; one man in the court rejects Elisha's words, providing the lesson.

> *Then Elisha said, Hear ye the word of the LORD; Thus saith the LORD, Tomorrow about this time shall a measure of fine flour be sold for a shekel, and two measures of barley for a shekel, in the gate of Samaria. Then a lord on whose hand the king leaned answered the man of God, and said, Behold, if the LORD would make windows in heaven, might this thing be? And he said, Behold, thou shalt see it with thine eyes, but shalt not eat of it.*   2 Kings 7:1-2

A few desperate guys stagger out to the Syrian army, calculating if they stay in the city they'll die of famine. The Lord used these guys to chase off the Syrian army — they only discover remnants as the army fled. As they return and report, the king sends out a patrol and finds the invaders gone.

## Chapter Three

*And the people went out, and spoiled the tents of the Syrians. So a measure of fine flour was sold for a shekel, and two measures of barley for a shekel, according to the word of the LORD. And the king appointed the lord on whose hand he leaned to have the charge of the gate: and the people trod upon him in the gate, and he died, as the man of God had said, who spoke when the king came down to him. And it came to pass as the man of God had spoken to the king, saying, Two measures of barley for a shekel, and a measure of fine flour for a shekel, shall be tomorrow about this time in the gate of Samaria.*
2 Kings 7:16-18

Events unfold as the Lord said, even in a situation appearing hopeless. Remember our guys in Daniel 3 — they faced an uncertain outcome, but knew God would either deliver them from death, or through it. There's no guarantee of an easy life, or healing, or anything else, only God's plan is better than we could hope for.

You may say, I understand all that — God is with us, He has His best in mind for us, and so on, but when two people go to the doctor each hears the same news: It's cancer. Yet one is cured and the other is terminal. Two people go to school — one is killed by a nutcase, the other isn't. In those times doubt sets in on God's plan, exactly as it did for the disciples in Mark 4.

That's not fair! How can a loving God allow such tragedy? School shootings, attacks on innocents, crime and violence generally. Why won't God heal everyone? Why doesn't God do something? Doesn't He care we're perishing? Why does God allow suffering? Or why do bad things happen to good people?

God says all have sinned and fallen short of the glory of God. From God's view all are sinners and in need of repentance; all have fallen short, all need forgiveness. This universe isn't what God intended. Way back on page one, God created and called it good. Yet by page two, Adam appears and scrambles the whole planet. Entropy starts, and decay, sin, and corruption enter the world. Before sin, the world was perfect. After, it's corrupting day by day.

Never forget this world isn't what God intended. He uses events for our learning and to work for good (Romans 8:28), but don't look for understanding because this world is fallen, corrupted, and sinful. Man caused this fallen state, not God, and reaps what he sows. Satan's greatest deception shifts blame to God for his work. You've seen insurance policies saying they don't cover "acts of God." Yet read Job's story, who was to blame for his problems?

Shifting blame could be Satan's greatest strategy. Don't fall for it — this world isn't what God intended.

Through it all these guys knew God was able to deliver, and even if He didn't save them from death, God has a superior plan. That's the trust we need to develop. If you're going through tough times, consider a few verses you can cling to.

> *While we look not at the things which are seen, but at the things which are not seen: for the things which are seen are temporal; but the things which are not seen are eternal.*
> 2 Corinthians 4:18

> *For God hath not given us the spirit of fear; but of power, and of love, and of a sound mind.*  2 Timothy 1:7

> *For I know the thoughts that I think toward you, saith the LORD, thoughts of peace, and not of evil, to give you an expected end.*  Jeremiah 29:11

> *For my thoughts are not your thoughts, neither are your ways my ways, saith the LORD. For as the heavens are higher than the earth, so are my ways higher than your ways, and my thoughts than your thoughts.*  Isaiah 55:8-9

> *Behold, I am the LORD, the God of all flesh: is there any thing too hard for me?*  Jeremiah 32:27

> *Thus saith the LORD; Refrain thy voice from weeping, and thine eyes from tears: for thy work shall be rewarded, saith the LORD; and they shall come again from the land of the enemy. And there is hope in thine end, saith the LORD, that thy children shall come again to their own border.*
> Jeremiah 31:16-17

A simple lesson learned from chapter 3 — my God can deliver, and even if He doesn't, I won't bow to fear, or man, or the world because I'm anchored to a rock stronger than me. God will deliver me from death and disaster or through it. Either way, His plan always proves superior over anything we can imagine. Don't quit, don't give in.

So what do you think Nebuchadnezzar thought after bold statements from these Hebrews?

# Chapter Three

> *Then was Nebuchadnezzar full of fury, and the form of his visage was changed against Shadrach, Meshach, and Abednego; therefore he spoke, and commanded that they should heat the furnace seven times more than it was usually heated.*
> Daniel 3:19

This had to be scary and intimidating — a few lone men refusing the king's order and Nebuchadnezzar responds with anger and hatred, commanding to heat the furnace seven times more than normal. Seven times means completely hot; as hot as they could get it. They couldn't raise the temperature seven times hotter, but seven in the Bible speaks of completeness; as hot as possible.

A clay kiln operates from 1,000 to 1,500 degrees (in round numbers). To make pottery the potter grabs a lump of clay and forms it on a wheel to obtain the shape, then places it into extreme heat hardening the vessel into something useful. If you dig up clay and allow it to dry, adding water returns it to clay; by exposing it to extreme heat, irreversible changes occur making the clay useful for other purposes.

If we asked the pot, would it be fun? I don't think so. Do you see the parallel? God allows trials to lead to maturity, strength, and durability, and those changes become irreversible. We need those qualities and they come from the fire.

> *And he commanded the most mighty men that were in his army to bind Shadrach, Meshach, and Abednego, and to cast them into the burning fiery furnace.*
> Daniel 3:20

Not tossed into, but bound as well. Nebuchadnezzar prefers to avoid taking chances.

> *Then these men were bound in their coats, their stockings, and their turbans, and their other garments, and were cast into the midst of the burning fiery furnace.*
> Daniel 3:21

Nothing left behind. Nothing to remind him of their testimony. The king wants to erase them from history, like Orwell's "unperson."

> *... an Unperson is someone who has been vaporized. Vaporization is when a person is secretly murdered and erased from society, the present, the universe, and existence. Such a person would be taken out of books, photographs, and articles so that no trace of them is found in the present anywhere – no record of*

*them would be found. This was so that a person who defied the Party would be gone from all citizens' memories, even friends and family.*\*

God's people ought to be salt and different from the crowd. Salt exhibits many properties, but it can be an irritant, a preservative, and purifier. Some people don't like reminders of the truth and seek to eliminate any trace of existence.

*Therefore because the king's commandment was urgent, and the furnace exceeding hot, the flame of the fire slew those men that took up Shadrach, Meshach, and Abednego.*   Daniel 3:22

It's so hot they couldn't get near. Clay kilns fire around 1,000 degrees or so, and this fire was as hot as they could make it; you couldn't come close without severe problems.

*And these three men, Shadrach, Meshach, and Abednego, fell down bound into the midst of the burning fiery furnace.*
Daniel 3:22

They fell into the fire as the guys holding them vaporize. The end of our heroes. At least they stood firm. What were they thinking? How long did it take to realize God preserved them? Did they have final doubts? Perhaps they thought, this is it, I guess God isn't going to save us.

*Doubt is normal; we need to build faith. Biblical faith differs from what today we call "blind faith," or hope, faith in biblical terms "means that persuasion is not the outcome of imagination but is based on fact, such as the reality of the resurrection of Christ, and as such it becomes the basis of realistic hope."*†

It's the faith we have in bridges over a river — it's concrete and steel. While we haven't undertaken an analysis of the concrete and steel it's a reasonable expectation based on knowledge of construction (you don't drive off the bank and hope you'll fly to the other side). That's what the Bible means by faith — it's a faith based on reason and facts. Study what the Bible says on faith in Hebrews 11.

---

\*   Anonymous (2021)
†   Zodhiates (1992a, page 1162)

## Chapter Three

*Through faith we understand that the worlds were framed by the word of God, so that things which are seen were not made of things which do appear.*   Hebrews 11:3

Paul speaks of atoms (and quarks, gluons, leptons and fermions). In Romans 1:19–20 Paul states the creation itself testifies of God. It's a reasonable conclusion when you examine the universe. God created the universe, and the evidence surrounds us.

*And what shall I more say? For the time would fail me to tell of Gideon, and of Barak, and of Samson, and of Jephthah; of David also, and Samuel, and of the prophets; Who through faith subdued kingdoms, wrought righteousness, obtained promises, stopped the mouths of lions, Quenched the violence of fire, escaped the edge of the sword, out of weakness were made strong, became valiant in fight, turned to flight the armies of the aliens.*   Hebrews 11:32–34

You say, gee that's great. If I have faith, it all works out, right? That's the error of faith teachers claiming God wants everyone to be rich, have a big house, and a Lexus (with ice cream and a pony). But keep reading.

*And others had trial of cruel mockings and scourgings, yea, moreover of bonds and imprisonment; They were stoned, they were sawn asunder, were tested, were slain with the sword; they wandered about in sheepskins and goatskins; being destitute, afflicted, tormented; (Of whom the world was not worthy:) they wandered in deserts, and in mountains, and in dens and caves of the earth.*   Hebrews 11:36–38

Others in Greek means another of a different kind. These were not delivered as those in the previous verses were. Yet they displayed faith as well. Not everyone is healed. Not all are rich. Not everyone has a Lexus. Or ice cream. Or a pony.

Faith teachers do a disservice to the church — not only from corrupt doctrine, but their error leads to problems if you believe God always heals if you have enough faith. What happens if you're not healed? Either you lacked faith, or God isn't listening. Either result is wrong. Did Paul lack faith when he asked for his malady to be removed? I don't think so. God answered My grace is sufficient, and it has to be.

We are to ask God, but must accept the answer. And no is an answer, but one we don't like. Not all are healed — why isn't everyone? I don't know. Trust is hard when you're unsure and don't know the outcome. These guys in Daniel didn't know what was going to happen. Perhaps they thought this is it.

But it wasn't.

> *Then Nebuchadnezzar the king was astounded, and rose up in haste, and spoke, and said unto his counselors, Did not we cast three men bound into the midst of the fire? They answered and said unto the king, True, O king.* Daniel 3:24

Of course they're not alone. You're never alone in trials, Satan wants you to think you are. Remember the disciples from Mark chapter 4 — they traveled with the creator of the universe yet were still afraid. We have the same advantage they had; the creator of the universe travels with us as well. Do we act like it?

> *He answered and said, Lo, I see four men loose, walking in the midst of the fire, and they have no hurt; and the form of the fourth is like the Son of God.* Daniel 3:25

Who joined them in the fire? Jesus Himself. Recall Isaiah 43 — *when* you go through the fire.

There's an old poster of a person walking along a beach, with footprints visible in the sand. The person speaks to Jesus as he looks back over his life and the footprints. "Lord, I see two sets of footprints all through my life, but during the worst, most dark times, there's only one set. Why did you leave me when I needed you most?" And the Lord replies, "It was during those times I carried you."

You are never alone, even though sometimes it feels that way. One reason we often return to the story of the disciples in the boat in Mark 4 — at one time we've all been there. We've all had doubts. We've all wondered where God was as the waves crash over the bow. We've all thought we've been abandoned.

But you haven't. No matter what it feels like.

> *Then Nebuchadnezzar came near to the mouth of the burning fiery furnace, and spoke, and said, Shadrach, Meshach, and Abednego, ye servants of the most high God, come forth, and come here. Then Shadrach, Meshach, and Abednego, came forth of the midst of the fire.* Daniel 3:26

# Chapter Three

Nebuchadnezzar undergoes a rapid change of heart. As we've seen, he is impressionable and easily changes his mind. But this time our heroes honor his request. These guys didn't want to "stick it to the man," but the king's previous order was one they could not follow as it involved worship of false gods (idols).

> *And the princes, governors, and captains, and the king's counselors, being gathered together, saw these men, upon whose bodies the fire had no power, nor was an hair of their head singed, neither were their coats changed, nor the smell of fire had passed on them.* Daniel 3:27

The fire has no power — the guy that created it controls it. You hold an appointed number of days and nothing can stop or terminate them short of completion. It could be today or fifty years away, we don't know. But if the Lord still has work for you to accomplish, no fire can cut those days short. Of course, this doesn't mean to tempt God by being foolish, but in your service to the Lord you can be sure your mission will be completed. You don't know what completed means to the Lord, it could be someone else comes along and your time is done. In short, do your best to stay safe and avoid dangerous situations.

> *Then Nebuchadnezzar spoke, and said, Blessed be the God of Shadrach, Meshach, and Abednego, who hath sent his angel, and delivered his servants that trusted in him, and have changed the king's word, and yielded their bodies, that they might not serve nor worship any god, except their own God.* Daniel 3:28

Nebuchadnezzar praises them for sticking to God.

> *Therefore I make a decree, That every people, nation, and language, which speak any thing amiss against the God of Shadrach, Meshach, and Abednego, shall be cut in pieces, and their houses shall be made a refuse heap; because there is no other God that can deliver after this sort.* Daniel 3:29

Nebuchadnezzar didn't quite understand the grace part of God. He understood the power, but forgot forgiveness and longsuffering of God.

> *Then the king promoted Shadrach, Meshach, and Abednego, in the province of Babylon.* Daniel 3:30

Where was Daniel during these events? You're left with three choices.

1. If present, he bowed down to the idol? Based on what we know about Daniel it's unlikely.
2. Present but not accused? Again, not likely. He'll have a plan hatched against him in a few chapters, so it's unlikely his enemies would skip a chance to eliminate him.
3. Or not present? The likely scenario. Daniel was probably on an affair for the state and wasn't present, and the bad guys seized the opportunity to attack his friends.

Daniel's absence provides a model for the church and the tribulation. Some were not present (Daniel) some were preserved through, some died in. Another clue the church will not experience the tribulation. Consider Noah and the flood — some were preserved through, some perished in, and some were taken out before (Enoch was pre-flood).

We need to absorb the lessons of Daniel. Paul writes in Romans 15 these stories are preserved for our learning — do we avail ourselves of the lessons herein? It's much easier to learn from the story than be doomed to repeat it for yourself.

*Chapter 5*

# Chapter Four

PEOPLE REFUSE TO HEED warnings — you see them standing on the train track with the engine coming and they won't get out of the way; you can only stand and watch the wreck. In this chapter Daniel provides Nebuchadnezzar a warning, who ignores it until God explains it to him a little more clearly.

Nebuchadnezzar pens this chapter himself for distribution throughout the known world. Although a slow learner, the King wants everyone to benefit from his experience. As we shall see in later chapters, his sons don't heed his warnings and refuse to learn the lessons. History repeats itself, again.

> *Nebuchadnezzar the king, unto all people, nations, and languages, that dwell in all the earth; Peace be multiplied unto you.*
> Daniel 4:1

Nebuchadnezzar was the most powerful man in the world, conquering the known world. At that time, if a king defeated another nation it meant his gods overpowered theirs. Since Nebuchadnezzar defeated the whole world he felt he was most powerful, and his gods more powerful than any other. But he'll soon learn a lesson.

> *I thought it good to show the signs and wonders that the high God hath wrought toward me. How great are his signs! And how mighty are his wonders! His kingdom is an everlasting kingdom, and his dominion is from generation to generation.*
> Daniel 4:2–3

Nebuchadnezzar reflects back on his lessons. At this point he believes in God, but was he sincere? Did his commitment to God continue? Commentators disagree — some believe he was saved, others not. It's easy to make a commitment to God under high emotions, but do commitments continue after the situation ends?

Remember the parable of the sower in Matthew 13. Some seed falls on good ground and grows, other falls on shallow soil and after it begins to grow withers in the sun due to its poor foundation. But nothing is wrong with the seed — it's the same for both soils. Did Nebuchadnezzar continue with his commitment to God? We don't know.

Nebuchadnezzar changes his mind often — he's impressionable and easily swayed (not a good characteristic); you must have confidence in your convictions and not allow yourself to be swayed. Don't be bull-headed and inflexible, but also don't allow circumstance to dictate your beliefs, and don't bother with what others do. You may be all alone, but that doesn't matter if you're on the right side; right and wrong can't be determined by a vote.

> *I Nebuchadnezzar was at rest in mine house, and flourishing in my palace.* Daniel 4:4

Nebuchadnezzar did that a lot — sit back and relax in his palace. After all, he conquered the world, the stock market performed well, he had plenty of food and wine, what else did he need? But if you have too much stuff, you might think you've earned it or done something to deserve it. It also makes you rely on your stuff instead of God. You may be blessed by God, but don't allow your blessings to be your downfall.

> *But godliness with contentment is great gain. For we brought nothing into this world, and it is certain we can carry nothing out. And having food and raiment let us be therewith content. But they that will be rich fall into temptation and a snare, and into many foolish and hurtful lusts, which drown men in destruction and perdition.* 1 Timothy 6:6-9

> *He that loveth silver shall not be satisfied with silver; nor he that loveth abundance with increase; this is also vanity.* Ecclesiastes 5:10

Be content with what you have. Possessions bless some, others not as they can be a snare. Whether you have a little or a lot, be content with it. Consider Paul at the end of his life, he said whatever state he was in, he was content. As he was in jail and about to be executed, it would have been easy to be bitter over

# Chapter Four

his life — he gave up considerable social status to follow Christ, dying with nothing; Paul considered all worldly things as a loss to gain Christ.

> *I saw a dream which made me afraid, and the thoughts upon my bed and the visions of my head troubled me.*   Daniel 4:5

Yogi Bera said it's deja vu all over again; haven't we seen this before? Sounds like earlier in Daniel's book doesn't it? Man doesn't learn from history — the only thing we learn from history is man learns nothing from history, and Nebuchadnezzar didn't learn from his past either.

It might be surprising to see God speak to the gentile king; as God used Balaam's donkey, He uses anyone He wishes however He wishes. Don't limit God to this group or that group. He possesses unlimited power and resources and uses anyone and anything He wants to accomplish His goals. God provides a warning specifically for him. Nebuchadnezzar shows his problem in verses one through five as he uses the words I-my-me ten times! Nebuchadnezzar's problem was it's all about me; as King, nobody will tell him any different.

> *Therefore made I a decree to bring in all the wise men of Babylon before me, that they might make known unto me the interpretation of the dream.*   Daniel 4:6

Daniel wasn't in the group this time; perhaps he neared retirement (some commentators say this could be twenty years after the previous chapter). But for whatever reason the other guys had the first opportunity, and of course fail.

> *Then came in the magicians, the astrologers, the Chaldeans, and the soothsayers; and I told the dream before them; but they did not make known unto me the interpretation thereof.*
> Daniel 4:7

Either they couldn't, or wouldn't as they feared the meaning. If they did understand and feared to tell the king the meaning, what good are they as advisers? Surrounding yourself with people who won't speak the truth is worthless.

> *But at the last Daniel came in before me, whose name was Belteshazzar, according to the name of my god, and in whom is the spirit of the holy gods, and before him I told the dream, saying*
> Daniel 4:8

Nebuchadnezzar uses Daniel's Hebrew name, as well as the name given to him in Babylon. That's a large honor, as the captives received new names after being taken. Even after all these years, Daniel's Hebrew name hasn't been lost, and the King uses it as a sign of respect towards Daniel (don't confuse Daniel/Belteshazzar with Nebuchadnezzar's grandson Belshazzar appearing in the next chapter).

> *O Belteshazzar, master of the magicians, because I know that the spirit of the holy gods is in thee, and no secret troubleth thee, tell me the visions of my dream that I have seen, and the interpretation thereof.*
> Daniel 4:9

Chief of magicians doesn't mean Daniel suddenly turned pagan, it's the Babylonian job title. As we've learned from Daniel's character, he would never compromise. Daniel and Nebuchadnezzar enjoyed a special relationship — he knew Daniel would speak the straight scoop in contrast to other advisers only telling the king what he wanted to hear.

> *Thus were the visions of mine head in my bed; I saw, and behold a tree in the midst of the earth, and the height thereof was great. The tree grew, and was strong, and the height thereof reached unto heaven, and the sight thereof to the end of all the earth. The leaves thereof were fair, and the fruit thereof much, and in it was food for all; the beasts of the field had shadow under it, and the fowls of the heaven dwelt in the boughs thereof, and all flesh was fed of it.*
>
> *I saw in the visions of my head upon my bed, and, behold, a watcher and an holy one came down from heaven; He cried aloud, and said thus, Hew down the tree, and cut off his branches, shake off his leaves, and scatter his fruit; let the beasts get away from under it, and the fowls from his branches. Nevertheless leave the stump of his roots in the earth, even with a band of iron and bronze, in the tender grass of the field; and let it be wet with the dew of heaven, and let his portion be with the beasts in the grass of the earth. Let his heart be changed from man's, and let a beast's heart be given unto him; and let seven times pass over him.*
>
> *This matter is by the decree of the watchers, and the demand by the word of the holy ones, to the intent that the living may know that the most High ruleth in the kingdom of men, and giveth it*

## Chapter Four

> *to whomsoever he will, and setteth up over it the basest of men.*
> Daniel 4:10–17

That's the dream, and he didn't understand it. You can see how it might be disturbing — even without the understanding, it's not a pretty picture.

> *This dream I king Nebuchadnezzar have seen. Now thou, O Belteshazzar, declare the interpretation thereof, forasmuch as all the wise men of my kingdom are not able to make known unto me the interpretation; but thou art able; for the spirit of the holy gods is in thee.* Daniel 4:18

Nebuchadnezzar knew Daniel would speak the truth even if not popular. Too many times Christians fear to speak up afraid of being offensive. Truth isn't always popular, and if you withhold the truth for fear of being offensive you're not being a good friend, or parent.

It would be popular to tell the king this dream provides abundant blessing, but wouldn't be true. Read 1 Kings 22 as a warning of what happens when people don't speak the truth. Sadly, many churches want to be "seeker-friendly," and instead of proclaiming man's sin and need for a savior, they preach church potlucks and ice cream. That's not only wrong, it's a huge disservice for people who will end up in hell for lack of proper teaching.

Sometimes the truth isn't popular. Daniel understood the dream's meaning, pausing before telling the king what it meant. Daniel and Nebuchadnezzar must have been close, and the king respected Daniel not only for his ability, but for speaking the truth even when it wasn't pleasant.

> *Then Daniel, whose name was Belteshazzar, was perplexed for one hour, and his thoughts troubled him. The king spoke, and said, Belteshazzar, let not the dream, or the interpretation thereof, trouble thee. Belteshazzar answered and said, My lord, the dream be to them that hate thee, and the interpretation thereof to thine enemies.* Daniel 4:19

Daniel's astonishment arose not because he didn't know the dream, but because he did. After composing himself, Daniel proceeds to tell the king the meaning he seeks.

> *The tree that thou sawest, which grew, and was strong, whose height reached unto the heaven, and the sight thereof to all*

> *the earth; Whose leaves were fair, and the fruit thereof much, and in it was food for all; under which the beasts of the field dwelt, and upon whose branches the fowls of the heaven had their habitation: It is thou, O king, that art grown and become strong: for thy greatness is grown, and reacheth unto heaven, and thy dominion to the end of the earth.* Daniel 4:20-22

Similar to his previous dream, the head of gold represents Nebuchadnezzar, the pinnacle of human government.

> *And whereas the king saw a watcher and an holy one coming down from heaven, and saying, Hew the tree down, and destroy it; yet leave the stump of the roots thereof in the earth, even with a band of iron and bronze, in the tender grass of the field; and let it be wet with the dew of heaven, and let his portion be with the beasts of the field, till seven times pass over him;* Daniel 4:23

Nebuchadnezzar loses the kingdom for seven years. As a hint, it's the same reason God destroyed Sodom.

> *Behold, this was the iniquity of thy sister Sodom, pride, fullness of bread, and abundance of idleness was in her and in her daughters, neither did she strengthen the hand of the poor and needy. And they were haughty, and committed abomination before me; therefore I took them away as I saw good.* Ezekiel 16:49-50

Pride is a big problem, perhaps because it was the first sin. People believe Sodom was destroyed for its sexual perversion. That is true, but notice the order of the list. Pride appears first, too many possessions comes second, too much leisure time last, resulting in not using your leisure time well.

Pride creeps in as you use gifts God gives you. Each Christian has at least one spiritual gift — an area God uniquely qualified you for ministry. But those gifts can become a source of pride. For this reason, don't ever tell someone they did a great job, since the skills are a gift from God — He could just as easy give those skills to someone else. Yet it's vital to encourage people; the best way acknowledges the source of the gift is from God.

Pride comes in two forms. First, obvious boasting about accomplishments and skills. But you might not realize people appearing humble are full of pride. What? Consider the person always downcast, saying they're nothing and can't do anything. My, what

## Chapter Four

humility we think! Yet God says you're something, and if you think you're nothing you're calling God a liar, and that's not humility, that's pride. CS Lewis wrote about it in "The Screwtape Letters."

> *MY DEAR WORMWOOD,*
>
> *I see only one thing to do at the moment. Your patient has become humble; have you drawn his attention to the fact? All virtues are less formidable to us once the man is aware that he has them, but this is specially true of humility. Catch him at the moment when he is really poor in spirit and smuggle into his mind the gratifying reflection, "By jove! I'm being humble," and almost immediately pride—pride at his own humility— will appear. If he awakes to the danger and tries to smother this new form of pride, make him proud of his attempt—and so on, through as many stages as you please.*
>
> *... By this method thousands of humans have been brought to think that humility means pretty women trying to believe they are ugly and clever men trying to believe they are fools. And since what they are trying to believe may, in some cases, be manifest nonsense, they cannot succeed in believing it and we have the chance of keeping their minds endlessly revolving on themselves in an effort to achieve the impossible.*
>
> *To anticipate the Enemy's strategy, we must consider His aims. The Enemy wants to bring the man to a state of mind in which he could design the best cathedral in the world, and know it to be the best, and rejoice in the fact, without being any more (or less) or otherwise glad at having done it than he would be if it had been done by another.*\*

The book reveals a series of letters between one of Satan's associates and his protege trying to drag a poor soul to hell. It contains revelations of Satan's strategies, one of which is pride. Notice Satan doesn't care which way you're off (he doesn't hold to anything specifically), as long as you're away from God's truth. As such, either excessive pride *or* false humility works for his aims.

> *This is the interpretation, O king, and this is the decree of the most High, which is come upon my lord the king: That they shall drive thee from men, and thy dwelling shall be with the beasts of the field, and they shall make thee to eat grass as oxen, and they shall wet thee with the dew of heaven, and seven*

---

\*    Lewis (1990, page 71–73)

> *times shall pass over thee, till thou know that the most High ruleth in the kingdom of men, and giveth it to whomsoever he will. And whereas they commanded to leave the stump of the tree roots; thy kingdom shall be sure unto thee, after that thou shalt have known that the heavens do rule.*   Daniel 4:24-26

Nebuchadnezzar needs to learn a lesson, but even with the warning he doesn't get it — occasionally we learn the hard way as man learns nothing from the past and repeats it. How about us? Nebuchadnezzar didn't learn the lessons, but do we? How often do we repeat mistakes of the past? The narratives in the Bible aren't quaint history, they provide lessons for us to learn from — we need to avail ourselves of the lessons contained therein.

Nebuchadnezzar was stubborn, but there's good stubborn and bad stubborn (that might surprise you). Good stubbornness we saw last chapter — not yielding even though everyone else does and you stand all alone. That's good character and confidence in what you *know* is true. Bad stubborn refuses teaching and warning, and that's the king's primary problem here.

> *Wherefore, O king, let my counsel be acceptable unto thee, and break off thy sins by righteousness, and thine iniquities by showing mercy to the poor; if it may be a lengthening of thy tranquility.*   Daniel 4:27

Daniel warns the King and advises him to change his path. Jonah warned the people of Nineveh God's destruction was soon to fall on the city, but the king of Nineveh proclaimed a fast, saying who knows if God will relent and spare the city. Daniel wonders if Nebuchadnezzar changes his way if this judgment will pass by. But the king does nothing, refusing to change as time goes by.

The train wrecks coming. Repent or be judged. Judgment doesn't come to the king for months; likely he's forgotten what Daniel said. But don't mistake the long-suffering of God for the approval of God. God hasn't forgotten, you're not getting by with it and God most certainly doesn't approve. God doesn't change, and neither does His word. What's true then remains true today. *Because sentence against an evil work is not executed speedily, therefore the heart of the sons of men is fully set in them to do evil.* (Ecclesiastes 8:11)

> *All this came upon the king Nebuchadnezzar. At the end of twelve months he walked in the palace of the kingdom of Babylon.*   Daniel 4:28-29

He's about to make a big mistake; he never learned the lesson Daniel tried to give him, and the king bears responsibility for his actions. People say if God wanted to, He would stop me. After all, if it was *really* bad, and God is all-powerful, why doesn't God prevent me from sinning in the first place? Because God allows choice — you don't have to follow Him. God provides time for repentance, but don't mistake time for approval.

Consider Noah and the flood. Noah worked on that boat for decades before the flood came. God gave people a witness to what would occur, and allowed time for repentance. But in all those years, how many were saved? Zero. Noah was a failure. But there he is, in the great "Hall of Faith" in Hebrews 11. God doesn't judge by results, but by obedience. You do what God calls you to do, and leave the results to Him.

> *The king spoke, and said, Is not this great Babylon, that I have built for the house of the kingdom by the might of my power, and for the honor of my majesty?* Daniel 4:30

Whoops. The king makes a big mistake; it *was* a great city, but who gave it to him? Recall Jeremiah 28 if you need a refresher. God gave all this to Nebuchadnezzar, and the king steals the glory for himself, instead of giving it to God. And that's too far — judgment comes.

> *While the word was in the king's mouth, there fell a voice from heaven, saying, O king Nebuchadnezzar, to thee it is spoken; The kingdom is departed from thee. And they shall drive thee from men, and thy dwelling shall be with the beasts of the field: they shall make thee to eat grass as oxen, and seven times shall pass over thee, until thou know that the most High ruleth in the kingdom of men, and giveth it to whomsoever he will.* Daniel 4:31–32

He should have listened. A year went by for opportunity to learn the lesson Daniel spoke, but ignored it. God allows a chance for repentance, but be assured, eventually judgment comes.

> *The same hour was the thing fulfilled upon Nebuchadnezzar, and he was driven from men, and did eat grass as oxen, and his body was wet with the dew of heaven, till his hairs were grown like eagles' feathers, and his nails like birds' claws.* Daniel 4:33

Most commentators believe the king was afflicted with some psychological problem, perhaps temporary insanity.

> *And at the end of the days I Nebuchadnezzar lifted up mine eyes unto heaven, and mine understanding returned unto me, and I blessed the most High, and I praised and honored him that liveth for ever, whose dominion is an everlasting dominion, and his kingdom is from generation to generation:*
> Daniel 4:34

For him to return to his throne is amazing, but it started with taking the focus off himself. When he takes the focus off himself and looks to heaven, his sanity returns and he resumes his royal duties.

> *And all the inhabitants of the earth are reputed as nothing; and he doeth according to his will in the army of heaven, and among the inhabitants of the earth; and none can stay his hand, or say unto him, What doest thou? At the same time my reason returned unto me; and for the glory of my kingdom, mine honor and brightness returned unto me; and my counselors and my lords sought unto me; and I was established in my kingdom, and excellent majesty was added unto me. Now I Nebuchadnezzar praise and extol and honor the King of heaven, all whose works are truth, and his ways justice; and those that walk in pride he is able to abase.*
> Daniel 4:35-37

Nebuchadnezzar learns his lesson (at least temporarily). We can benefit from others' mistakes. But the only thing we learn from history is man learns nothing from history as the same mistakes repeat over and over. Where does that leave us?

> *Thus saith the LORD, Let not the wise man glory in his wisdom, neither let the mighty man glory in his might, let not the rich man glory in his riches; But let him that glorieth glory in this, that he understandeth and knoweth me, that I am the LORD which exercise lovingkindness, judgment, and righteousness in the earth; for in these things I delight, saith the LORD.*
> Jeremiah 9:23-24

> *Two things have I required of thee; deny me them not before I die; Remove far from me vanity and lies; give me neither poverty nor riches; feed me with food convenient for me; Lest I be full, and deny thee, and say, Who is the LORD? Or lest I be*

## Chapter Four

*poor, and steal, and take the name of my God in vain*
Proverbs 30:7–9

Learn the lesson or you're doomed to repeat it.

*Except the LORD build the house, they labor in vain that build it: except the LORD keep the city, the watchman waketh but in vain.*
Psalm 127:1

*Chapter 6*

# Chapter Five

IN PREVIOUS CHAPTERS Nebuchadnezzar's pride overcame him, and God explained to him the problems of pride a little more clearly, but do his children listen? Do they avail themselves of lessons from their father? Sadly not, as this chapter repeats Nebuchadnezzar's previous lessons — the only thing we learn from history is man learns nothing from history; people don't avail themselves of learning from previous mistakes.

> *Belshazzar the king made a great feast to a thousand of his lords, and drank wine before the thousand.* Daniel 5:1

Belshazzar is Nebuchadnezzar's grandson (don't confuse Belshazzar with Belteshazzar which is another name for Daniel). Nebuchadnezzar died about 562 BC and now his grandson commands Babylon. The kingdom deteriorated after Nebuchadnezzar's death, and this night the enemy approaches the gate — the Persian army surrounds Babylon.

During a time of siege a commander prepares defenses and plots strategy. But not Belshazzar as he expressed overconfidence in Babylon and its defenses. A mistake as we shall see, but not entirely unfounded as a river ran through the city supplying water, and the city held considerable stockpiles of food (some believe as much as a twenty-year supply). With these defenses and supplies, most believed the city impossible to conquer. Yet the Bible contains prophecy the city would be overthrown; Belshazzar would be wise to consider the situation instead of throwing a party.

Two common mistakes occur in these situations, and both prove fatal — not preparing before, and trusting in your preparations. Don't believe anyone claiming you should ignore reasonable precautions as a situation develops because God will take care of it. Nowhere in the Bible do we see anyone ignore reasonable preparations when facing difficult situations. But the second problem is as bad as the first, the error of trusting in your preparations.

After doing all you can to prepare, know ultimate protection arrives from the Lord. Proverbs states the horse is prepared for the day of battle, but safety is from the Lord; don't rely on yourself or your preparations, as pride causes big problems for the Christian.

> *Belshazzar, while he tasted the wine, commanded to bring the golden and silver vessels which his father Nebuchadnezzar had taken out of the temple which was in Jerusalem, that the king, and his princes, his wives, and his concubines, might drink from them.* Daniel 5:2

Nebuchadnezzar seized the temple instruments after conquering the city, but showed respect by keeping them preserved, while his grandson shows no such respect and orders them removed to serve his guests. Why would Belshazzar do this? Drunk? Or Pride and trying to show his supremacy? Either way he's gone too far, and God executes judgment on Belshazzar for his wanton disobedience.

Don't mistake the longsuffering of God for God's approval. You're not getting away with your sin, and God hasn't forgotten about you. God's longsuffering provides opportunity for repentance, but if people remain stiff-necked and refuse to repent judgment *will* come.

> *Then they brought the golden vessels that were taken out of the temple of the house of God which was at Jerusalem; and the king, and his princes, his wives, and his concubines, drank from them.* Daniel 5:3

Drunkenness allows you to take actions you wouldn't normally do, which causes trouble. This does not mean if you have a glass of wine you're doomed to eternal damnation, but consuming too much alcohol never leads to anything good. For those thinking Christians should *never* drink, remember Jesus made wine in John chapter 2, and Paul advised Timothy to take some wine for his stomach ailments. It's not the alcohol, it's the abuse of it causing problems. It's not bad because it's sin, it's sin because it's bad.

Recall the Jews in the Old Testament and many of the regulations regarding food and sanitary conditions; on the surface they didn't make much sense (at least to the people of the time). Yet today we understand many provide basic sanitary or other benefits. God didn't make a bunch of rules to be mean, He did it for their protection.

Adultery, murder, drunkenness, and pride are not sin because God wants to deprive you of fun, but sin because they're bad. It doesn't matter if you're a Christian or not, these are universally bad.

> *They drank wine, and praised the gods of gold, and of silver, of bronze, of iron, of wood, and of stone.*      Daniel 5:4

Sounds like a modern Hollywood awards ceremony, doesn't it? If you've seen Hollywood shows, all they do is proclaim how great they are or make political statements. In one awards show, Kathy Griffin said after winning for her show:

> *"A lot of people come up here and thank Jesus for this award. I want you to know that no one had less to do with this award than Jesus," an exultant Griffin said, holding up her statuette. "Suck it, Jesus. This award is my god now."* *

Ms. Griffin's god is a chunk of plastic and metal — nothing changed in thousands of years since man first worshiped hunks of wood. In Daniel's time pagans worshiped gods of metal and wood, and today people still do (they've added plastic to the metal and wood). We may not bow down to an altar in our home, but people worship idols nonetheless; an idol replaces God, exactly what Ms. Griffin states she's done.

Babylon was polytheistic (gods for the sun, moon, wind, rain and so on), so any god would do, and if you had a god they would be happy to add it to their worship — after all, you didn't want to anger a god you might need later. But Isaiah states the wisdom of worshiping blocks of wood.

> *He burneth part thereof in the fire; with part thereof he eateth flesh; he roasteth roast, and is satisfied; yea, he warmeth himself, and saith, Aha, I am warm, I have seen the fire; and the residue thereof he maketh a god, even his carved image; he falleth down unto it, and worshippeth it, and prayeth unto it, and*

---

\*    Reuters (2007)

*saith, Deliver me; for thou art my god. They have not known nor understood; for he hath shut their eyes, that they cannot see; and their hearts, that they cannot understand.*
                                                                Isaiah 44:16-18

It's amazing what people worship. Man begins life with an innate desire to worship and acknowledge something exists higher than him. Confusion results over discovering the true god, and while people choose the wrong god, at least they understand something is out there — we're not all a cosmic accident.

Today we worship chance (evolution). From the goo to the zoo to you; man's arrogance denies the existence of any god at all. Unfortunately evolution is unscientific, and atheism is illogical. To state no god exists you must possess all knowledge; if you don't have all knowledge god can exist outside of what you know. Proudly proclaiming themselves an atheist states for all the world they lack critical thinking skills and logic.

For logical and critical thinking people, it's not the existence of God (since atheism is illogical), but how big is your God? Is it a hunk of wood? Can it hear? Can it respond? Does it need to be rescued? In the story of Laban in Genesis 31 as he chases down Jacob, he states it's bad you took my daughters, but did you have to steal my gods? Can your god be stolen? Or scratched?

*In the same hour came forth fingers of a man's hand, and wrote over against the lampstand upon the plaster of the wall of the king's palace; and the king saw the part of the hand that wrote.*
                                                                Daniel 5:5

God is long-suffering but you're not getting by with it; He hasn't forgotten and He doesn't approve. Sin is sin. Period. Sin thousands of years ago remains sin today. God doesn't change — don't believe the lie the Bible must be "re-interpreted" in light of today. Bull. It was true then, it's true and unchanged today. Certainly an all-knowing and all-powerful God understood differences between society thousands of years ago and today, and has the ability to communicate timeless truths.

God hasn't changed, man has as he desires to approve previously unacceptable acts. And it's still sin. You're free to reject what God says and act as you please, but you're not free to restate what God said. Sin is sin. Yesterday and today (and tomorrow). If you only accept parts of the Bible you like, you've created your own designer religion.

## Chapter Five

Due to the King's sin, he sees a hand appear and write on the wall (a phrase we still use today), creating fear and trembling. As both Hebrew and Aramaic read right to left, how was it laid out on the wall? In a line like this:
S R P L K T N M N M
Or as most think, vertically like this?

| P | T | M | M |
|---|---|---|---|
| R | K | N | N |
| S | L |   |   |

Or vertically backward?

| S | L | N | N |
|---|---|---|---|
| R | K | M | M |
| P | T |   |   |

It's unsure how the letters appeared on the wall, but we'd imagine seeing the hand write sobered up the king quickly.

> *Then the king's countenance was changed, and his thoughts troubled him, so that the joints of his loins were loosed, and his knees smote one against another.*     Daniel 5:6

That's polite old King James English requiring a little explaining — remember how your mother told you when you left the house to be sure you had clean underwear in case you were in an accident? The king experienced an accident but no car was involved. And now you better understand what the polite King James implies in verse 6, as the king calls his magicians to explain what the writing means, hopefully settling down his restless knees.

> *The king cried aloud to bring in the astrologers, the Chaldeans, and the soothsayers. And the king spoke, and said to the wise men of Babylon, whosoever shall read this writing, and show me the interpretation thereof, shall be clothed with scarlet, and have a chain of gold about his neck, and shall be the third ruler in the kingdom.*     Daniel 5:7

He sobered up quick. We've seen this story before with Nebuchadnezzar and his dream, and we already know no adviser can provide the king what he needs.

*Then came in all the king's wise men; but they could not read the writing, nor make known to the king the interpretation thereof. Then was king Belshazzar greatly troubled, and his countenance was changed in him, and his lords were perplexed.*                                                                                         Daniel 5:8-9

Aramaic infers vowels, so several possibilities exist for their failure to comprehend the message. Not only could the writing be vertical, but several words can be formed, with several meanings.

- Mene could mean "mina" (50 shekels) or the word numbered.
- Tekel could mean "shekel" (1 shekel) or weighed.
- Peres (singular of upharsin) could mean half-sheckel, half mina or divided. It can also mean Persia.

Even if they could decipher the words, they might read this as 101 shekels and the meaning escapes them. So they're puzzled and fail to provide the king the meaning; only God can provide the king what he desires.

*Now the queen, by reason of the words of the king and his lords, came into the banquet house; and the queen spoke and said, O king, live for ever; let not thy thoughts trouble thee, nor let thy countenance be changed.*                                                                                       Daniel 5:10

The Queen is likely Nebuchadnezzar's widow, and she's seen this act before. She recalls Daniel provided Nebuchadnezzar understanding after the failure of magicians in a similar situation, and she knows Daniel can do it again, so she advises the king Daniel is the man he seeks.

*There is a man in thy kingdom, in whom is the spirit of the holy gods; and in the days of thy father light and understanding and wisdom, like the wisdom of the gods, was found in him; whom the king Nebuchadnezzar thy father, the king, I say, thy father, made master of the magicians, astrologers, Chaldeans, and soothsayers;*                                                                                          Daniel 5:11

Quite a build-up for Daniel from the Queen as she knew Daniel and events of the past, and relates to the King a summary of his skills.

*Forasmuch as an excellent spirit, and knowledge, and understanding, interpreting of dreams, and revealing of hard sentences, and dissolving of doubts, were found in the same Daniel, whom the king named Belteshazzar; now let Daniel be called, and he will show the interpretation.*     Daniel 5:12

The Queen addressed Daniel by his Hebrew name, showing considerable respect as Daniel lived a captive of Babylon for decades and been given a new name.

*Then was Daniel brought in before the king. And the king spoke and said unto Daniel, art thou that Daniel, which art of the children of the captivity of Judah, whom the king my father brought out of Jewry? I have even heard of thee, that the spirit of the gods is in thee, and that light and understanding and excellent wisdom is found in thee.*     Daniel 5:13-14

Daniel likely lived in retirement when summoned by the King (being over eighty years old). But you never retire in your service to God. Don't ever think you're too old to be of use to God — you're never too old and never retire. God can use anyone anytime; Daniel hasn't lost his edge.

Daniel's reputation preceded him before the king; your reputation always precedes you, either good or bad. If you lie and cheat, people will know. If you live as an honest person (as much as possible), people will know.

*Walking east on Jefferson Street with the setting sun behind him, Abraham Lincoln followed his shadow toward the house on Sixth Street where he had arranged to meet his love in secret. The tall man cast a long shadow in the November light. ... The outline of a silver maple against the sky was delicate but firm; the network of shades the branches cast upon the ground seemed to him a virtual "profile" of the tree. "Perhaps a man's character is like a tree, and his reputation like its shadow; the shadow is what we think of it; the tree is the real thing."* \*

Honest Abe provides a valuable lesson. It's easy to be consumed by your reputation and what others might think about you (or gossip behind your back). Yet we shouldn't concern ourselves with gossip, but character and integrity — other people may or may not see the correct shadow, but your character casts the shadow, not the other way around.

---

\*     Epstein (2008)

*And now the wise men, the astrologers, have been brought in before me, that they should read this writing, and make known unto me the interpretation of it but they could not show the interpretation of the thing. And I have heard of thee, that thou canst make interpretations, and dissolve doubts: now if thou canst read the writing, and make known to me the interpretation thereof, thou shalt be clothed with scarlet, and have a chain of gold about thy neck, and shalt be the third ruler in the kingdom.*  Daniel 5:15–16

As earlier with Nebuchadnezzar, the wise men of the world fail. Only the true God can get the job done. Nebuchadnezzar exposed the wise men as frauds, unable to perform when it mattered since they served gods made of metal and wood and unable to communicate or save. No block of wood can answer. No idol can speak.

A quick glance of ancient gods worshiped included Ashtoreth, Baal, Mammon, Molech and Nebo. We don't worship those anymore — we've grown beyond them right? Look at their gods and see if they're still worshiped today.

- Ashtoreth — Pleasure and sexuality. It's good for me, and it doesn't matter who gets hurt as long as my needs are met.
- Baal — Power. Looking at any recent presidential race proves many still worship Baal.
- Mammon — Money. Wall Street is filled with people worshiping Mammon as greed runs rampant in society. Nothing is ever enough.
- Molech — Practicality. Molech existed as a statue with arms outstretched and worshipers built a fire in his belly until he glowed red-hot; the idea if you sacrificed your first child Molech would honor your sacrifice and bless you. It was practical to sacrifice one to be blessed. Surely we don't do such hideous acts today? Today we use salt water instead of fire and call it planned parenthood. If you sacrifice your first child, you'll have a better career and be better able to take care of your next child.
- Nebo — God of knowledge and wisdom. Take a walk on any college campus and you'll still see this god bowed down to daily.

Where do you place your trust? What are you worshiping? The ancient gods still hang around, but we're more stealthy in their worship. When it comes down to it, who do you trust? Your money? Your knowledge? Or the true and living God?

When you call on Baal, or Mammon, or Nebo, nothing answers as money, power, and wisdom can't save you. You may not bow to an idol, but where do you place your trust? You need to know because you become like the gods you worship.

> *The idols of the heathen are silver and gold, the work of men's hands. They have mouths, but they speak not; eyes have they, but they see not; they have ears, but they hear not; neither is there any breath in their mouths. They that make them are like unto them; so is every one that trusteth in them*
> Psalm 145:15-18

Is your god cold and unfeeling? You'll become that way. Is your god insensitive?

> *Then Daniel answered and said before the king, let thy gifts be to thyself, and give thy rewards to another; yet I will read the writing unto the king, and make known to him the interpretation.*
> Daniel 5:17

Look back to chapter 1 as Daniel purposed in his heart not to defile himself, a commitment standing decades later in his eighties (a reminder you need to make your commitment now. When you're under pressure it's too late to decide which way to go).

Daniel avoids material temptation, but before the interpretation, he first provides a public service announcement; he enjoys a captive audience and it's a good time for a lesson. The king likely didn't want to listen, but had no choice — only Daniel could provide the information he needed, so Daniel avails himself of the teaching moment.

In a respectful way, Daniel lets the king have it. Speak the truth and don't be a jerk, but don't hold back either. Too many people error in one of two ways; first, the "sandwich-board" approach screaming out "the end is near" turning people away. Second, the person refraining from speaking the truth to avoid offending anyone. Both approaches are wrong. Speak the truth in love, but don't be a jerk.

> *O thou king, the most high God gave Nebuchadnezzar thy father a kingdom, and majesty, and glory, and honor; and for the majesty that he gave him, all people, nations, and languages, trembled and feared before him. Whom he would he slew; and*

*whom he would he kept alive; and whom he would he set up; and whom he would he put down.* Daniel 5:18-19

Nebuchadnezzar was the head of Gold and the pinnacle of government; every kingdom following his was inferior. The story begins well, but notice the buts in Daniel's message. It's always a bad thing when a story starts well, and then the dreaded "but" comes up.

*But when his heart was lifted up, and his mind hardened in pride, he was deposed from his kingly throne, and they took his glory from him. And he was driven from the sons of men; and his heart was made like the beasts, and his dwelling was with the wild asses; they fed him with grass like oxen, and his body was wet with the dew of heaven; till he knew that the most high God ruled in the kingdom of men, and that he appointeth over it whomsoever he will.* Daniel 5:20-21

A summary of the previous chapter, and history they all would know as Daniel provides a reminder of pride's problems, something Belshazzar should have been aware of.

*And thou his son, O Belshazzar, hast not humbled thine heart, though thou knewest all this;* Daniel 5:22

Nebuchadnezzar boasted in his accomplishments resulting from God's actions. He continued in his pride until God explained Himself a little more clearly. Belshazzar insults God himself by using the temple instruments and failed to learn from history. His fall will be worse than his father's.

*But hast lifted up thyself against the Lord of heaven; and they have brought the vessels of his house before thee, and thou, and thy lords, thy wives, and thy concubines, have drunk wine in them; and thou hast praised the gods of silver, and gold, of bronze, iron, wood, and stone, which see not, nor hear, nor know; and the God in whose hand thy breath is, and whose are all thy ways, hast thou not glorified.* Daniel 5:23

Belshazzar had the benefit of his grandfather's experience but didn't learn. He made a choice to avoid the lessons from his father and do it his own way. We face the same situation; Paul reminds us the stories in the Bible aren't random acts, they provide lessons for us; we must avail ourselves of the lessons or be doomed to repeat the same mistakes.

# Chapter Five

> *Then was the part of the hand sent from him; and this writing was written.*
> Daniel 5:24

Judgment comes; at some point the Lord always judges. He allows ample time for repentance, but you're not getting by. Don't confuse the longsuffering of God with forgetfulness, or worse, acceptance. Sin is sin, always has been, always will be. God doesn't change. The Bible can't be "re-interpreted" for a new age (conveniently calling many popular acts permissible).

> *And this is the writing that was written, MENE, MENE, TEKEL, UPHARSIN.*
> Daniel 5:25

We've noted why this might have been difficult to understand, but Daniel completes his lesson and now moves to give the King what he desperately wanted: the meaning.

> *This is the interpretation of the thing: MENE; God hath numbered thy kingdom, and finished it.*
> Daniel 5:26

Your number's up (another phrase still used today). God allowed Belshazzar time to repent, and he didn't so judgment comes. A time comes when no more chances exist. God is longsuffering, merciful and just, but don't assume He will not judge. A righteous God *must* judge or He can't be righteous. To ignore sin is not righteous, but God always allows time for repentance before judgment.

God has a number in mind; Proverbs 16:33 states the lot is in lap of the Lord. It turns out randomness is hard to find anywhere in the cosmos. A staggering problem in computer science involves finding random numbers, which may not appear interesting, but as you understand cryptography bases its security on it, the lack of randomness becomes a stubbornly large and persistent security issue. Actual randomness remains a stubborn illusion.

We have a finite number of days — what are we doing with them? Do we use them for God's glory, or squander them? You could die today, tomorrow, or fifty years from now; use whatever time you have profitably (Psalm 90:12).

> *TEKEL; Thou art weighed in the balances, and art found wanting.*
> Daniel 5:27

Judgment comes for everyone. For some at the great white throne in Revelation, but for Christians it's a report card on how they used the resources God gave them. Recall the parable of the servants, some were provided many talents, another one. The master didn't expect them all to perform the same, but he did expect them all to use what they had. You're not judged by how others perform, but by how you use what God gave you.

Consider the churches in Revelation, many of which didn't measure up, but each thought they were doing differently than they really were. The churches believing they were doing well had considerable problems, and the ones believing they were in bad shape didn't have many faults.

> *PERES; Thy kingdom is divided, and given to the Medes and Persians.* Daniel 5:28

Peres is the singular form of upharsin, and also a pun for Persia. Look back to the image Nebuchadnezzar saw — the chest represented Persia. The fall of Babylon to the Persians is certain, and Daniel recalled the image given to Nebuchadnezzar earlier.

> *Then commanded Belshazzar, and they clothed Daniel with scarlet, and put a chain of gold about his neck, and made a proclamation concerning him, that he should be the third ruler in the kingdom.* Daniel 5:29

The King is relieved he knows, and gives Daniel gifts. Unknown to him, the Persian army outside the walls of the city diverted the river and were preparing to walk under the walls and into the city to conquer it. Belshazzar in his pride and arrogance lost Babylon as the Persians took the city without any consequential battle.

> *In that night was Belshazzar the king of the Chaldeans slain.* Daniel 5:30

Don't confuse the fall of Babylon in 539 BC with the destruction of Babylon. Even many scholars try to place the destruction of Babylon here when the Persians took over, but a casual reading of Isaiah displays difficulties.

> *And Babylon, the glory of kingdoms, the beauty of the Chaldees' excellency, shall be as when God overthrew Sodom and Gomorrah. It shall never be inhabited, neither shall it be dwelt in from generation to generation; neither shall the Arabian pitch tent there; neither shall the shepherds make their fold there.* Isaiah 13:19–20

Obviously that hasn't happened yet. The fall of Babylon occurs in 539 BC to the Persians, while the destruction awaits a future time.

> *And Darius the Median took the kingdom, being about threescore and two years old.*                                        Daniel 5:31

The Persians take over, and according to legend, when Cyrus walked into the city Daniel met him with a scroll of Isaiah where God Himself writes a letter to Cyrus in Isaiah 45:1, detailing his exploits and conquests, making an impression on him.

*Chapter 7*

---

## Chapter Six
---

> *It pleased Darius to set over the kingdom an hundred and twenty princes, which should be over the whole kingdom; and over these three presidents; of whom Daniel was first; that the princes might give accounts unto them, and the king should have no damage.* Daniel 6:1-2

No executive can handle affairs themselves — the King appoints others to oversee portions of the kingdom, as the President appoints people to delegate to. Darius appoints 120 cabinet members, with one person over each forty reporting directly to him. Unfortunately, if those turn out to be unsavory people the administration has problems.

It's an issue of stewardship — these guys weren't faithful to the king or their position; only Daniel displayed loyalty to the king. In a trusted position, it's easy to pilfer from the treasury, but since Daniel won't go along with the theft, they become jealous of Daniel and need to remove him.

> *Then this Daniel was preferred above the presidents and princes, because an excellent spirit was in him; and the king thought to set him over the whole realm.* Daniel 6:3

Daniel rises above others, so the king desires to put him in charge. This seriously impairs their ability to skim off the top, so Daniel has to go. Political games haven't changed much, have they?

Daniel rose to the top in the new administration; just as in Nebuchadnezzar's cabinet, he's now at the top of the Persian administration. As Daniel takes over the remaining guys don't like it; they weren't honest, and verse 2 hints they were ripping off the king. If Daniel stays, it's likely their crimes would become known, so they devise a scheme to eliminate Daniel.

> *Then the presidents and princes sought to find occasion against Daniel concerning the kingdom; but they could find none occasion nor fault; forasmuch as he was faithful, neither was there any error or fault found in him.* Daniel 6:4

One problem with their plan — Daniel's closet contained no skeletons to exploit; a true definition of integrity and honesty. Political investigations uncover "youthful indiscretions" to be exploited to your advantage; Daniel didn't have dirt to dig up, so a new plan must be hatched.

> *Then said these men, we shall not find any occasion against this Daniel, except we find it against him concerning the law of his God.* Daniel 6:5

Daniel didn't have any dirt — amazing for a man approaching eighty years old. No "youthful indiscretions" in his past, and we know from chapter 1 Daniel's devotion and commitment to God — Daniel's integrity thwarted their plan as the enemies of Daniel admit his integrity; as Judas admitted Jesus was innocent, the enemies admit Daniel lacks faults. It's one thing for friends to testify of your integrity, it's another after constant searching for weaknesses your enemies themselves admit to your honesty.

> *Then these presidents and princes assembled together to the king, and said thus unto him, King Darius, live for ever. All the presidents of the kingdom, the governors, and the princes, the counselors, and the captains, have consulted together to establish a royal statute, and to make a firm decree, that whosoever shall ask a petition of any god or man for thirty days, except of thee, O king, he shall be cast into the den of lions.* Daniel 6:6-7

*All* the presidents of the kingdom? They're lying of course, as Daniel would not agree. These are not honorable men; they're only interested in continuing their looting. They need to find a way to distract the king from their true motives, and they hatch a perfect plan — appeal to his pride!

Pride might be the first sin and what caused Satan's downfall. It's the problem with Sodom and Gomorrah (Ezekiel 16:49), and remains a problem today. Satan knows how easily man falls for pride and arrogance, and no one is immune — it's a perfect plan to con the King to perform their bidding.

> *Now, O king, establish the decree, and sign the writing, that it be not changed, according to the law of the Medes and Persians, which altereth not. Wherefore king Darius signed the writing and the decree.*  Daniel 6:8–9

Hasty decisions are usually bad. If you're pressured for a decision, it's likely you're facing unintended consequences. That's not always true, but don't yield to situations pushing you in a certain direction *right now*; if the decision is correct it can wait a short time while you ensure it's the correct move.

Early in the book of Acts as the disciples discuss Judas' departure, they must select a replacement. Narrowing the choices down to two, they ask God to pick one of the two (by casting lots). Did God direct them to do it? Nope. They were rushed to do *something*, and instead of waiting on the Lord made a hasty decision.

The Persian kingdom was inferior to Nebuchadnezzar's who held ultimate authority over life and laws. Nebuchadnezzar made laws, and retracted laws. The Persian king could not reverse a law once signed, which is why this scam worked; had these guys attempted the same on Nebuchadnezzar it would have failed.

Recall Esther chapter 8 where a similar situation plays out. The king could not reverse the decree stating all Jews were to be killed, but he could provide for their defense, and even decree they could appropriate property of anyone who attacked them (Esther 8:10–11). Thus, while technically the decree to exterminate the Jews remained in force, it was practically nullified by the King's legal moves.

> *Now when Daniel knew that the writing was signed, he went into his house;*  Daniel 6:10a

It's important to note what Daniel *didn't* do. He didn't organize a protest or mail-writing campaign. He simply went home. Often we get sidetracked on political issues; you should be involved in political matters (not just presidential races) — check out where the candidates stand and pick one most closely aligning with biblical views and morals. Protests and other political games don't accomplish much; even if Daniel protested, nothing would come of it as the law could not be changed.

Christians should be involved, but don't become over consumed by politics (and mixing politics and the church remains a big no-no). Daniel understood the situation would not change, so he returns home as normal. It's simply mind over matter — Daniel doesn't mind, so their ridiculous law doesn't matter.

> ... *and his windows being open in his chamber toward Jerusalem, he kneeled upon his knees three times a day, and prayed, and gave thanks before his God, as he did previously.*
> Daniel 6:10b

Daniel neither opened nor closed his windows — he neither calls attention to himself nor hides, he continues his normal routine. Daniel demonstrated balance. He could pray in secret, and who would have blamed him? It's only 30 days.

But he's a leader, and holds higher duty and responsibility. Daniel was accountable to a higher standard, and he accepted ignoring the law could land him in big trouble. Christians are called to obey governmental authority unless it contradicts God's law. But be it known, if you choose to disobey laws you'll likely face unpleasant consequences.

Why would Daniel have his windows toward Jerusalem? The city lies in rubble, and Daniel spent over sixty years away from the city. Why maintain this? The answer comes from 1 Kings.

> *If they sin against thee, (for there is no man that sinneth not), and thou be angry with them, and deliver them to the enemy, so that they carry them away captives unto the land of the enemy, far or near; yet if they shall take it to their hearts in the land where they were carried captives, and repent, and make supplication unto thee in the land of them that carried them captives, saying, we have sinned, and have done perversely, we have committed wickedness; and so return unto thee with all their heart, and with all their soul, in the land of their enemies, which led them away captive, and pray unto thee toward their land, which thou gavest unto their fathers, the city which thou hast chosen, and the house which I have built for thy name; then hear thou their prayer and their supplication in heaven thy dwelling place, and maintain their cause.*   1 Kings 8:46-49

Daniel prays for the city and his people. Notice Daniel takes the Bible literally; it's not an allegory or allusion. At the beginning of chapter 9 as Daniel reads Jeremiah, he knows the captivity nears its end. He didn't wonder what Jeremiah meant by seventy years — it means a period of time (seventy years). So Daniel knew the time neared ending, and prays for the people as in 1 Kings.

It's important to take your Bible at face value. Many asked what does it mean when the Bible says Israel will be back in the land? After scattering for 2,000 years, how could they be regathered back in the land? So "scholars" questioned God's Word, spouting different interpretations to those passages — some leading to replacement theology (where the church replaced Israel in God's plan, and that's all you need to know about it as not only is it untrue, it's heresy). They wondered about the meaning of Israel until 1948, when (just as God said), Israel returned to the land God gave them.

> *Then these men assembled, and found Daniel praying and making supplication before his God.*     Daniel 6:11

The guys waited for Daniel as they knew he would not yield. That shows the strength of Daniel's commitment — his enemies testify of Daniel's character as they know he would never compromise.

> *Then they came near, and spoke before the king concerning the king's decree; hast thou not signed a decree, that every man that shall ask a petition of any god or man within thirty days, save of thee, O king, shall be cast into the den of lions? The king answered and said, the thing is true, according to the law of the Medes and Persians, which altereth not.*     Daniel 6:12

They first ask, did you sign the law King? If the King hasn't signed it, they don't want to continue since they're working a scam, and don't want to tip their hand it's an attack against Daniel.

> *Then answered they and said before the king, that Daniel, which is of the children of the captivity of Judah, regardeth not thee, O king, nor the decree that thou hast signed, but maketh his petition three times a day.*     Daniel 6:13

Now they spring the trap. As a leftover from the previous administration, they view Daniel as inferior, and his integrity interferes with their ripping off the king, so he's got to go.

> *Then the king, when he heard these words, was very much displeased with himself, and set his heart on Daniel to deliver him; and he labored till the going down of the sun to deliver him.*     Daniel 6:14

The king can't change law, but he struggles to find a workaround. It's likely his lawyers worked on it, but they were unable to find a resolution. The King didn't pass the buck, he's upset with *himself* for being scammed; he easily could have blamed the responsible parties, but the King knows he bears responsibility.

That's a lost art (taking responsibility). Harry Truman's famous sign "The Buck stops here" represents an attitude passing long ago. The one thing a politician doesn't want to do is take a stand on anything, or accept responsibility. It's pass the hot potato, and avoid responsibility at all costs.

> *Then these men assembled unto the king, and said unto the king, Know, O king, that the law of the Medes and Persians is, that no decree nor statute which the king establisheth may be changed.* Daniel 6:15

They remind the king no way out exists; the law can't be changed. Quite brave of them since the king could easily remove them as well. The law couldn't be changed as they believed the king to be a form of deity, and god doesn't make mistakes, thus if the king signs a law it must be good; the scam works on the king by appealing to his pride.

> *Then the king commanded, and they brought Daniel, and cast him into the den of lions. Now the king spoke and said unto Daniel, thy God whom thou servest continually, he will deliver thee.* Daniel 6:16

A pagan king states God wants to deliver Daniel, but is He able? Pagans believed god wanted to intervene, the question was, did they have the power? Not all gods were equal; their gods weren't all-powerful and the question always was *can* their god perform? Yet Christians know our God *is* all-powerful; we say God is able, but will He? We want it our way, all the time; a problem stemming from a lack of trust in God.

> *And a stone was brought, and laid upon the mouth of the den; and the king sealed it with his own signet, and with the signet of his lords; that the purpose might not be changed concerning Daniel.* Daniel 6:17

Two seals were set upon the den — the king's authority wasn't absolute.

# Chapter Six

*Then the king went to his palace, and passed the night fasting: neither were instruments of music brought before him; and his sleep went from him. Then the king arose very early in the morning, and went in haste unto the den of lions.*
Daniel 6:18–19

The king didn't know the outcome either. Was Daniel's God able? Did He have the ability to save him? After all, the king liked Daniel; he was upset at himself for allowing this travesty of justice to occur.

*And when he came to the den, he cried with a lamentable voice unto Daniel; and the king spoke and said to Daniel, O Daniel, servant of the living God, is thy God, whom thou servest continually, able to deliver thee from the lions?*
Daniel 6:20

God didn't spare Daniel *from* trials, but preserved Daniel *through* them. Nothing in the Bible promises an easy life; in fact the opposite as Jesus *guaranteed* problems in life. Return to chapter 3 and notice God *will* deliver, but maybe not how you want. God is not a genie you can wish upon — He's smarter and His plan is best, even if you don't see it right away.

Sometimes you must learn a lesson and no other way exists to learn it. "No pain, no gain" is the athlete's motto (which doesn't exactly match the idea here, but you get the idea); pain causes growth we desperately need. That doesn't make it fun or easy, but necessary.

*Then said Daniel unto the king, O king, live for ever.*
Daniel 6:21

Daniel provides an interesting response to the King. His first words were not GET ME OUT OF HERE, perhaps for two reasons. First, Daniel had peace that passes understanding. It's easy to ask why events occur, but it didn't bother Daniel. He trusted in God and knew whatever He planned was best. Thus, he wasn't in a rush if God had other plans. Many times we run around trying to do something, but sometimes don't just do something, stand there.

Daniel's peace came not *from* understanding. If you're looking for peace from understanding many times it will elude you. Many ask how could a loving God allow wars and disease? Or natural disasters? If a loving God existed, He would stop bad events from happening. Doesn't God care? Of course. But to the question of why God allows certain events, I've come to one answer:

I don't have the slightest idea.

And I've learned over the years nobody else does either. If you're looking for reasons, many times you won't find them. Many events in the world appear random or evil for no reason. Why allow it? I don't know. Scanning the first few chapters of Job it's obvious much occurs behind the scenes we're not involved in, and frequently unaware of.

The error with Job comes from thinking it answers the question of why the innocent suffer. If that's the case, the question is never answered. No, the book of Job requires obtaining the divine viewpoint. The first few chapters provide the background story, and then thirty chapters or so of Job's friends bloviating about this and that, but providing no answers. And then, God provides Job the divine viewpoint.

> *Moreover the LORD answered Job, and said, Shall he that contendeth with the Almighty instruct him? He that reproveth God, let him answer it. Then Job answered the LORD, and said, Behold, I am vile; what shall I answer thee? I will lay mine hand upon my mouth. Once have I spoken; but I will not answer; yea, twice; but I will proceed no further. Then answered the LORD unto Job out of the whirlwind, and said, Gird up thy loins now like a man; I will demand of thee, and declare thou unto me. Wilt thou also disannul my judgment? Wilt thou condemn me, that thou mayest be righteous? Hast thou an arm like God? Or canst thou thunder with a voice like him?*                 Job 40:1-9

And *that's* the divine viewpoint; if you understand you get the peace which *passes* understanding. But back to Daniel. He had company (besides the lions) and enjoyed the conversation.

> *My God hath sent his angel, and hath shut the lions' mouths, that they have not hurt me: forasmuch as before him innocency was found in me; and also before thee, O king, have I done no hurt.*        Daniel 6:22

Daniel points out to the king the unjust accusation. Daniel displays tact, but never compromises the truth. Even before the king holding the power of life and death if he didn't like what he heard, Daniel reminds the king he's innocent of these bogus charges.

# Chapter Six

Recall Paul in Ephesians chapter 6 and the breastplate of righteousness. Considerable misunderstanding exists, as many confuse God's righteousness as your righteousness, but that's not what Paul has in mind. God's righteousness imputes to us the moment we believe, yet as Paul speaks to Christians and mentions this armor you need to pick up, he must have something else in mind.

Paul relates the practical day-to-day living of a righteous life (as best we can). How many pastors have been removed for affairs? How many unsaved mention the hypocrisy of people in the church cheating on their wives and taxes? These people don't wear a suitable breastplate because they've decided not to pick it up.

The breastplate covered the vital organs of the chest, and a blow through it usually proved fatal. How many Christians neglect Paul's advice and destroy their ministry? How frequently do we see leaders fall by not living a life of integrity? That's the breastplate Paul speaks of, as he hints at earlier in Ephesians.

> *I therefore, the prisoner of the Lord, beseech you that ye walk worthy of the vocation wherewith ye are called,*   Ephesians 4:1

In general, consider the complete lack of ethics and responsibility in today's society — not only do we tolerate sin, we promote it. Isaiah speaks of those promoting sin by drawing it with a cart (Isaiah 5:18) — people *proud* of their sin and want everyone to know it. That's the society we live in. But sin is sin, and you *are* responsible for it.

People devoted to their spouse, honest on their tax returns and working sixty minutes for every hour provide fodder for the butt of comedians jokes; most people consider loyalty and integrity an outdated concept applying only to old-timers. We've lost track of what Paul writes in Ephesians — even in the church the divorce rate mirrors those outside the church, and so on.

Today mirrors the book of Judges as it ends "everyone did what was right in their own eyes," the motto for today as situational ethics and value relativism rule the day. But it's not true — right, wrong, and absolute truth *do* exist. It may be a popular theme today, but nobody believes value relativism. Tell them you're going to steal their car, because *your* ethics say it's okay and you'll find out they *do* accept moral absolutes.

A court decision in November 2007 shows the contortion required to make situational ethics work.

> *Texas laws allow the killing of a fetus to be prosecuted as murder, regardless of the stage of development, but the laws do not apply to abortions, the state's highest criminal court has ruled. ... The Texas court said abortion precedent was based on the premise that a woman wants the procedure.\**

First situational ethics, and now situational murder. If the woman *wants* her baby dead and intends to kill it, it's not murder. But if she's in an accident causing the death of the unborn child, the other person *can* be prosecuted. This is the strange situation you find yourself in claiming simultaneously a baby isn't a person, yet want to protect it — *sometimes.*

But who's with Daniel? The same guy from chapter 3 — Jesus. And that's what gives calm. With the Lord Himself with Daniel, no fear could exist; a tough lesson to learn, as the disciples face a similar situation but react differently.

In Mark 4:35–40 the disciples travel in a boat, and when a storm arises they panic and ask don't you care we're dying? Why are you sleeping? They desperately wake up Jesus and rebuke Him for what they perceive as a lack of caring. Jesus speaks two words and their trial ends; they were never in any danger, but they sure didn't act like it.

How many times do we feel like they did during trials? Lord, I'm dying here, don't you care? Do something. Have you forgotten me? Yet we possess the same advantage the disciples and Daniel did, but forget it just like the twelve did in that boat. None of this means events will work out the way you want; when God says you're going to the other side of the lake you can be sure you're going to the other side — of course, the condition you'll arrive in isn't guaranteed, and that's where we make our mistake.

Because He didn't promise an easy journey.

> *Then was the king exceeding glad for him, and commanded that they should take Daniel up out of the den. So Daniel was taken up out of the den, and no manner of hurt was found upon him, because he believed in his God.*     Daniel 6:23

Like chapter 3, God delivers Daniel completely.

> *And the king commanded, and they brought those men which had accused Daniel, and they cast them into the den of lions, them, their children, and their wives; and the lions had the*

---

\*    Times (2007)

## Chapter Six

> *mastery of them, and broke all their bones in pieces before they came at the bottom of the den.*   Daniel 6:24

In case you thought the lions were tame or not hungry and that's how Daniel survived, these guys didn't last long. You may say that's not fair, why do the families share their punishment? Sin affects people around you. No such "victimless" crimes exist like drugs and prostitution; your actions impact others around you; Romans 14:7 states no man lives to himself, and no man dies to himself. Don't think you're an island (with apologies to Simon and Garfunkel).

> *Then king Darius wrote unto all people, nations, and languages, that dwell in all the earth; Peace be multiplied unto you. I make a decree, That in every dominion of my kingdom men tremble and fear before the God of Daniel; for he is the living God, and steadfast for ever, and his kingdom that which shall not be destroyed, and his dominion shall be even unto the end. He delivereth and rescueth, and he worketh signs and wonders in heaven and in earth, who hath delivered Daniel from the power of the lions.*   Daniel 6:25–27

Similar to Nebuchadnezzar's proclamation, but neither king realized you can't *make* people follow God or do the right thing by mere proclamation without motivating them. They were misdirected, even if they had the right idea. The job is information, what people do with it is up to them. Don't try and play the Holy Spirit.

> *So this Daniel prospered in the reign of Darius, and in the reign of Cyrus the Persian.*   Daniel 6:28

Daniel rose to power in two governments over sixty years. Imagine today if a Presidential cabinet member remained in service when the Presidency changes political parties. It just won't happen. But Daniel's integrity allowed him to be a trusted adviser in successive administrations, as everyone witnessed his integrity and honesty.

*Chapter 8*

# Chapter Seven

IN CHAPTER 7 DANIEL'S BOOK SHIFTS from history to prophecy; the remainder of the book contains visions and future events, critical background before diving into Revelation. So buckle up, it's Mr. Daniel's wild ride — similar to Disneyland, but much more fun and relevant.

Chapter 7 parallels Nebuchadnezzar's visions of metallic images from chapter 2; in contrast Daniel sees the same kingdoms portrayed as beasts. Why the difference? The same events come from two different perspectives — chapter 2 contains *man's* view of kingdoms (shiny, valuable metals), chapter 7 displays *God's* view (voracious wild beasts). But the same governments appear in both chapters.

Many differences in the Bible (and apparent contradictions) become clear by understanding Einstein's relativity. If you've studied relativity a bit, you'll notice students always ask "which time is real" after computing the difference of two observations of the same event. My professor always grinned, and said: "it's relative — see, relativity isn't that hard" (and it's really not). Relativity means your observances may differ from others depending on where you sit.

Relativity explains why the age of the earth controversy isn't worth engaging in. Fifteen billion years only makes sense if you understand the reference frame involved — time is not absolute and varies. Additionally, if the speed of light slows over time, Physics will plunge into rapid change not seen since the turn of the century and Quantum Mechanics. Let's avoid all the controversial nonsense to settle on 15 billion years for the age of the universe.

Daniel chapters 2 and 7 appear different because the same events occur from two different points of view, similar to two different blind people describing an elephant, but one by the tail, the other by the snout. They express different descriptions of the same animal, yet the animal hasn't changed.

> *In the first year of Belshazzar king of Babylon Daniel had a dream and visions of his head upon his bed; then he wrote the dream, and told the sum of the matters.*     Daniel 7:1

This chapter precedes the events in chapter 6; don't make the mistake the Bible *always* presents events linearly — events can appear out of order and sometimes years skip by in a sentence. In the case of Daniel, the first six chapters document history, while the last six contain prophetic visions.

Daniel only presents the "sum of the matters," in other words, a summary. Elsewhere the Bible expands on these events (Revelation details the seventy weeks specifically, but we're ahead of ourselves) — you've got to do your homework. Too many people sit week after month in pews being spoon-fed and fail to do their homework. God raises up gifted teachers, but none substitute for performing your own research; don't be a lazy Christian.

It's not difficult to obtain a *basic* understanding of the entire Bible, paying dividends later — obtain a few quality commentaries and dig in! Both Jon Courson and Chuck Missler have audio commentaries on the entire Bible available (as well as Chuck Smith and many others). Load them onto your smartphone and you have a way to redeem the time, instead of listening to the latest techno music.

Four empires exist from Daniel's time until the end. That may be new to people unfamiliar with Bible prophecy but it's true; only four world empires ever existed — many nations tried for world dominion and failed. Germany (twice), England, Spain, and more all failed to gain the prize. Once again, what God said proves correct. Only four world empires will ever exist; we're still waiting on the last one (the revised Roman empire), but it won't be long now.

> *Daniel spoke and said, I saw in my vision by night, and, behold, the four winds of the heaven strove upon the great sea.*     Daniel 7:2

Portions of Daniel's vision contain code, but the Bible explains codes elsewhere. In this case, see Revelation 13:1–6 for a parallel section — even though thousands of years separate the writers, the Bible proves consistent (we call that the principle of expositional constancy, but that's a fancy name for the idea the Bible uses idioms consistently). Note the sea is an idiom for people (Isaiah 17:12-13, Revelation 13:1, Revelation 17:1, . . .).

> *And four great beasts came up from the sea, diverse one from another.* Daniel 7:3

These beasts represent four kingdoms until the end of history. How do we know? Vast amounts of scholarship and research? Nope. Read ahead and verse 17 of this chapter reveals exactly what the beasts represent. Many "scholars" make errors wasting time with vast research and theories, instead of reading their Bible. Frequently the Bible explains itself — no pseudo-scholarship needed. Don't be fooled by scholarship, do your own homework.

Each successive empire will be inferior to the previous; God says the cosmos is winding down — man is not getting better every day as some claim (the only reason to believe such nonsense is because evolution requires it, but common experience proves it not to be true). The principle of entropy holds for government as well as the cosmos.

> *The first was like a lion, and had eagle's wings; I beheld till the wings thereof were plucked, and it was lifted up from the earth, and made stand upon the feet as a man, and a man's heart was given to it.* Daniel 7:4

Babylon forms the head of gold from chapter 2, represented by an eagle. Babylon under Nebuchadnezzar created the pinnacle of human government. In chapter 2, inferior metals represent each successive kingdom. In chapter 7, the beasts become worse and more ferocious.

> *And behold another beast, a second, like to a bear, and it raised up itself on one side, and it had three ribs in the mouth of it between the teeth of it; and they said thus unto it, Arise, devour much flesh.* Daniel 7:5

The silver refers to the Medes and Persians, with three ribs representing three empires they conquered.

> *After this I beheld, and lo another, like a leopard, which had upon the back of it four wings of a fowl; the beast had also four heads; and dominion was given to it.* Daniel 7:6

Brass represents Alexander the Great. After his death the kingdom divides among his four generals before they're subsequently conquered.

> *After this I saw in the night visions, and behold a fourth beast, dreadful and terrible, and strong exceedingly; and it had great iron teeth; it devoured and broke in pieces, and stamped the residue with the feet of it; and it was diverse from all the beasts that were before it; and it had ten horns.* Daniel 7:7

Iron represents Rome. This vision contains ten horns, while chapter 2 lists feet of iron mixed with clay (ten toes). It's the same entity — God sees the action as continuous, while we see the intervening 2,000 years and separate kingdoms. That's the difference between chapter 2 and chapter 7, but don't be confused, they both speak of Rome, with the final phase being a ten-member confederacy.

Rome disintegrated but lived on in Europe — no nation ever conquered it, but decay set in from inside and it collapsed from corruption. It will re-emerge as a ten-nation confederacy, but it's the same kingdom.

> *I considered the horns, and, behold, there came up among them another little horn, before whom there were three of the first horns plucked up by the roots; and, behold, in this horn were eyes like the eyes of man, and a mouth speaking great things.* Daniel 7:8

A guy comes along, subdues three governments, unifying what's left under his totalitarian rule. We notice his great oratory skills, and his arrogance. This guy has many names, but the one we use (Antichrist) isn't a term the Bible uses much; Paul writes us a quick summary of this guy.

> *Let no man deceive you by any means; for that day shall not come, except there come the falling away first, and that man of sin be revealed, the son of perdition; Who opposeth and exalteth himself above all that is called God, or that is worshiped; so that he as God sitteth in the temple of God, showing himself that he is God. Remember ye not, that, when I was yet with you, I told you these things? And now ye know what withholdeth that he might be revealed in his time. For the mystery of iniquity doth already work; only he who now hindereth will continue to hinder, until he be taken out of the way. And then*

> *shall that Wicked be revealed, whom the Lord shall consume with the spirit of his mouth, and shall destroy with the brightness of his coming; Even him, whose coming is after the working of Satan with all power and signs and lying wonders.*
> 2 Thessalonians 2:3–9

He's also called the "Idol Shepherd" in Zechariah 11:17 — which lists a physical description of him. Don't spend too much time worrying over his identity; Paul says he won't be revealed until after the rapture. Besides, playing games with 666 and names fails to understand what occurs in Revelation 13, but we're *way* ahead of ourselves.

Unfortunately the pre-trib/post-trib discussion causes too many problems in the church. The post-trib people cite one error stemming from the pre-trib position — the tribulation following the rapture doesn't mean we escape persecution; life can get pretty bad before *the* great tribulation (note the definite article). The United States has (so far) not experienced the persecution most of the world has lived under for most of the last 2,000 years.

We fear the time of taking it easy will soon be over, as the dawn of the pandemic age revealed the church begins to turn on itself, with division and politics replacing ministry. How many post-pandemic-age pastors divide their membership over silly issues having nothing to do with the church? Don't be surprised when it occurs, and persecution *begins* with "pastors" and conventional churches and religious groups splitting and dividing over trivial issues they deem new doctrine. Calling them new Pharisees communicates the flavor of what lies over the horizon.

This guy won't run around with a pitchfork telling you he's the Antichrist; he's smart, politically savvy, and a shrewd negotiator (you have to be to get Jews and Muslims to agree on anything). Satan never identifies himself and says "I'm here to deceive you and rip you off." If he did that, you'd recognize it right off. Satan works stealthily; the whole idea of deception being you don't identify it.

You have to be on guard — deception is such because it's good and even has *some* truth to it. But mix a little cyanide with Kool-Aid and you're still dead — even though 99% of it is pure wholesome fruit juice and water with no artificial ingredients.

Cults and Satan mix a small amount of error with truth, but that's enough to cause considerable problems. Paul in Acts 16:17 delivers the damsel from her spirit of divination, as she followed Paul around crying these are servants of the most high God and show us the way of salvation. What she said was true, but mix 99% truth and 1% Drano and you're still dead — apparently she mixed in something beyond the truth, and Paul rebuked it.

How do you protect against deception? Not by intellect, or knowledge, or senses, but only by the word of God. Remember the words of Paul to the church at Galatia: if anyone preaches *anything* different from what Paul preached, let them be accursed — 90% right doesn't cut it. Cults can teach *mostly* truth; it's the remaining 5% that kills you.

The Antichrist (and Satan) are sneaky — he'll appeal and fool the whole world. Quite a feat since he'll appeal to Jews, Muslims, atheists, and so on. It's important to remember the Antichrist will be appealing, smart, and politically savvy (doubly important to know if you're on the earth during the great tribulation).

> *I beheld till the thrones were placed, and the Ancient of days did sit, whose garment was white as snow, and the hair of his head like the pure wool; his throne was like the fiery flame, and his wheels as burning fire. A fiery stream issued and came forth from before him; thousand thousands ministered unto him, and ten thousand times ten thousand stood before him; the judgment was set, and the books were opened.*
>
> Daniel 7:9–10

You may think we've jumped to Revelation, but no, we're still in Daniel; compare Revelation chapters 1,4–5 and note the consistency of idioms used in both places; even men writing thousands of years apart provide a unified message. You might take that for granted, but what other message across thousands of years uses the same idioms? A common image shows God's throne as fire — an interesting study comes from the first five times fire appears in the Bible.

- First mentioned in Genesis 15:17 — God's unilateral covenant with Abraham. God keeps his word, and the promises made to Abraham are still in effect (Genesis 12:3).
- Fire and brimstone in Genesis 19:24 — judgment.
- Genesis 22:6,7 — Abraham and Isaac and the sacrifice providing a model for man's redemption.
- Exodus 3:2 — God appears to Moses in the burning bush.
- Also Revelation 1:14, 2:18 — God is as fire.

*I beheld then because of the voice of the great words which the horn spoke; I beheld even till the beast was slain, and his*

*body destroyed, and given to the burning flame. As concerning the rest of the beasts, they had their dominion taken away; yet their lives were prolonged for a season and time.*
Daniel 7:11-12

Revelation chapter 19-20 details events briefly described here. Satan's downfall comes from pride; it landed him in trouble in the first place. Pride equally poisons the Christian; ask yourself why did God judge Sodom and Gomorrah? The answer commonly thought of isn't first; pride appears first (Ezekiel 16:49).

As usual, the world and God have different views; the world says you deserve a break and a Lexus (ice cream and a pony), while God in Luke 17:10 lays out His program, illustrating servants and their master. The servant is duty-bound to the master, and after performing all tasks shouldn't boast or look for rewards, after all "we are unprofitable servants; we have only done that which was our duty." Service is nothing to boast over, it's a Christian duty.

*I saw in the night visions, and, behold, one like the Son of man came with the clouds of heaven, and came to the Ancient of days, and they brought him near before him. And there was given him dominion, and glory, and a kingdom, that all people, nations, and languages, should serve him; his dominion is an everlasting dominion, which shall not pass away, and his kingdom that which shall not be destroyed.*
Daniel 7:13-14

From chapter 2 this is the stone cut without hands.

*I Daniel was grieved in my spirit in the midst of my body, and the visions of my head troubled me.*
Daniel 7:15

He didn't understand this; the vision must have provoked considerable thought. Many times prophecy isn't understandable until *after* it's fulfilled. Imagine Daniel (or John) seeing visions of the future with modern technology like tanks and planes — they would have no way of comprehending what they've seen, and little vocabulary to communicate with.

*I came near unto one of them that stood by, and asked him the truth of all this. So he told me, and made me know the interpretation of the things.*
Daniel 7:16

Daniel's confusion required him to ask about it. Even Peter said (when speaking of Paul's writings in 2 Peter 3:16) some ideas are hard to understand. Don't despair, when you're confused take it to God. Don't be as the disciples in Matthew 13 after Jesus speaks many parables, but only explains one. Jesus asks if they understand, and they reply yes. Of course they didn't, but they did fail to ask; due to their error the church for centuries argues the meaning of those parables.

> *These great beasts, which are four, are four kings, which shall arise out of the earth. But the saints of the most High shall take the kingdom, and possess the kingdom for ever, even for ever and ever.* Daniel 7:17-18

The good guys win. It doesn't always look like it, but the outcome is certain — the answers appear in the back of the book. Of course, the question is why do the evil prosper? Habakkuk expressed the same question, and it's a good review to understand God's perspective.

> *Then I would know the truth of the fourth beast, which was diverse from all the others, exceeding dreadful, whose teeth were of iron, and his nails of brass; which devoured, broke in pieces, and stamped the residue with his feet; And of the ten horns that were in his head, and of the other which came up, and before whom three fell; even of that horn that had eyes, and a mouth that spake very great things, whose look was more stout than his fellows.* Daniel 7:19-20

Notice the growth *out* of old Rome; no nation conquered it, it rotted from the inside. That's why God sees it as one continuous action, while man sees it separated by 2,000 years.

> *I beheld, and the same horn made war with the saints, and prevailed against them;* Daniel 7:21

This can't be the church as the gates of hell can't prevail against it (Matthew 16:18); confusion occurs in prophecy if you fail to understand the difference between Jews and the Church. Each holds a unique destiny to be fulfilled — make no mistake God is not finished with the Jews — you *must* understand this as we get to the 70-week prophecy or you'll be hopelessly lost.

A heresy arises since the Jews rejected Jesus the promises made to them are forfeit and now fall on the church. Not so. Study Genesis 15 as God's covenant with Abraham was unilateral, unconditional, and irrevocable — they can't forfeit it if they try.

The church is not Israel, and attempting to equate them leads to confusion and heresy.

It's true God appears to work with one group or the other, but not both simultaneously. From Abraham until Jesus, God worked with the Jews. From Jesus until the tribulation, it's the Church. After the rapture, God again works with the Jewish nation; they've been preserved over thousands of years and have a destiny to fulfill.

> *Until the Ancient of days came, and judgment was given to the saints of the most High; and the time came that the saints possessed the kingdom.* Daniel 7:22

The end of the book of Revelation with everything in time and according to plan. We may not like it, but when we gain understanding we'll agree His way was best.

> *Thus he said, The fourth beast shall be the fourth kingdom upon earth, which shall be diverse from all kingdoms, and shall devour the whole earth, and shall tread it down, and break it in pieces.* Daniel 7:23

The revised Roman empire makes its appearance, taking over the world again, this time with a singular leader.

> *And the ten horns out of this kingdom are ten kings that shall arise: and another shall rise after them; and he shall be diverse from the first, and he shall subdue three kings.* Daniel 7:24

The Antichrist puts together a confederacy of nations, subdues three, and consolidates power; Satan places his power in this guy.

> *And he shall speak great words against the most High, and shall wear out the saints of the most High, and think to change times and laws: and they shall be given into his hand until a time and times and the dividing of time.* Daniel 7:25

"Time and times and dividing of time" shows another way of saying three and one-half years. Don't ask what this means, it means a period of three and one-half years; those allegorizing the Bible have to decode the text, but if you accept what it says the meaning becomes obvious and clear; this time appears many different ways:

- 42 months — Revelation 11:2, 13:5
- 1,260 days — Revelation 11:3, 12:6
- Half of one week (literally "sevens") — Daniel 9:27
- Times, time and half a time (3 ½ years) — here and Daniel 12:7

Take your Bible literally and seriously. In Daniel 9 he recognizes by reading Jeremiah the captivity nears ending; Daniel never allegorizes the time period but understood the time exactly as Jeremiah wrote. Revelation isn't hard because it's unclear, but because it's clear and people don't like what it says.

> *But the judgment shall sit, and they shall take away his dominion, to consume and to destroy it unto the end. And the kingdom and dominion, and the greatness of the kingdom under the whole heaven, shall be given to the people of the saints of the most High, whose kingdom is an everlasting kingdom, and all dominions shall serve and obey him.*     Daniel 7:26-27

Every knee will bow. Even Satan knows his time is short, after all, he reads prophecy also. Interestingly, he takes it seriously and literally, ideas liberal "Christians" reject from their ignorance, to their downfall.

> *Here is the end of the matter. As for me Daniel, my cogitations much troubled me, and my countenance changed in me: but I kept the matter in my heart.*     Daniel 7:28

*Chapter 9*

# Chapter Eight

THE EVENTS OF CHAPTER 8 FOLLOW two years after chapter 7 (the first year of Belshazzar opens chapter 7). These visions parallel chapter 7, but with differences if studied carefully; chapters 2, 7, and 8 all contain visions of kingdoms with similar information, but described distinctly.

> *In the third year of the reign of king Belshazzar a vision appeared unto me, even unto me Daniel, after that which appeared unto me at the first.*
> Daniel 8:1

The following chart will assist in keeping things straight among the kingdoms and chapters in Daniel.

| Kingdom | Chapter 2 | Chapter 7 | Chapter 8 |
|---|---|---|---|
| Babylon | Gold | Lion | |
| Medo-Persia | Silver | Bear | Ram |
| Greece | Bronze | Leopard | Goat |
| Rome | Iron | Beast | |
| Antichrist | | | |

> *And I saw in a vision; and it came to pass, when I saw, that I was at Shushan in the palace, which is in the province of Elam; and I saw in a vision, and I was by the river of Ulai.*
> Daniel 8:2

This vision details kingdoms 2 & 3 — the Persians and Greeks only.

> *Then I lifted up mine eyes, and saw, and, behold, there stood before the river a ram which had two horns; and the two horns were high; but one was higher than the other, and the higher came up last.*  
> Daniel 8:3

The Ram represents the Medo-Persian empire (the bear from chapter 7, and the chest of silver from Nebuchadnezzar's dream in chapter 2). The Persians dominated over the Medes shown by this vision with one horn higher, and the bear with one side higher in the previous chapter. The same kingdom appears in both visions.

> *I saw the ram pushing westward, and northward, and southward; so that no beasts might stand before him, neither was there any that could deliver out of his hand; but he did according to his will, and became great. And as I was considering, behold, an he goat came from the west on the face of the whole earth, and touched not the ground; and the goat had a notable horn between his eyes.*  
> Daniel 8:4–5

The Persians (the bronze of chapter 2, and the leopard of chapter 7) conquered the world, but fell to Alexander the great of Greece, who became noted for his rapid conquest (conquering the world in a short span of years).

> *And he came to the ram that had two horns, which I had seen standing before the river, and ran unto him in the fury of his power. And I saw him come close unto the ram, and he was moved with anger against him, and smote the ram, and broke his two horns; and there was no power in the ram to stand before him, but he cast him down to the ground, and stamped upon him; and there was none that could deliver the ram out of his hand.*  
> Daniel 8:6–7

Alexander conquered the known world with incredible speed spreading the Greek language everywhere. Thus when Jesus arrives the world knows one language; the precision of Greek makes it perfect for New Testament writers. The conquests of Alexander worked for God's larger plan — Paul reminds us in Romans 8:28 *all* things work together for good, even if we don't understand it.

> *Therefore the he goat grew very great; and when he was strong, the great horn was broken; and for it came up four notable ones toward the four winds of heaven.*  
> Daniel 8:8

Alexander the Great dies after a drunken night, and the kingdom divides among his four generals. Notice the phrase *when he became strong, he fell*; pride and arrogance lead to his end. It's interesting you don't stumble in your weak areas, but the strong. For example, Peter's greatest characteristic was boldness — always action. Why did he deny the Lord? His boldness failed; his strongest characteristic.

If you're weak in one area you normally lean on the Lord for help. But in an area you think you've mastered, you attempt to handle it on your own. That's prideful, and what results in the fall. Be careful in the areas you think you don't have a problem in, they can spring up and trip you.

As a side note, Alexander died young due to his lifestyle. For people who think they're not hurting anyone by their actions (drug use, etc), Paul writes in Romans no one lives to himself, and no one dies to himself. Your actions (good or bad) impact others; Simon and Garfunkel were wrong — no one is an island.

> *I've built walls, A fortress deep and mighty, That none may penetrate. I have no need of friendship; friendship causes pain. It's laughter and it's loving I disdain. I am a rock, I am an island (Simon and Garfunkel "I am a Rock").*

All three empires (Babylonian, the Persian, and the Greek) go down in drunken parties. For those desiring to legalize drugs, have they not learned the lessons from the past? It appears not; the only thing man learns from history is man learns nothing from history — history repeats as mistakes repeat over and over.

> *The great empire of Alexander the Great went down because he was an alcoholic. He conquered the world, but he could not conquer Alexander the Great. There is a grave danger in Washington DC today, which is that many decisions are made during cocktail parties. Why do we think we are something special? Why are there people who think that the United States happens to be God's little pet nation?*\*

Is it acceptable for a Christian to drink? Can you have a glass of wine with your spaghetti, or a beer with your pizza during Monday night football? We're considering light drinking obviously; drunkenness is a problem referenced throughout the Bible —

---

\*   McGee (1982, page 579)

see Proverbs 20:1, Isaiah 5:11, Isaiah 28:7–8, 1 Peter 4:3 and 1 Corinthians 5:11.

It's not the alcohol causing problems, but drunkenness and allowing something to become a master over you. Alcohol is not evil by itself; Jesus Himself created wine (and Paul told Timothy to have a little wine for his stomach), so Christians are not required to be tea-totalers, but drunkenness leads to bad outcomes and is clearly excluded. As always, balance. It's acceptable to have wine, but excess is bad — if you can't control your consumption, don't do it at all.

> *And out of one of them came forth a little horn, which grew exceedingly great, toward the south, and toward the east, and toward the pleasant land.* Daniel 8:9

He sounds like the guy from the last chapter, but read the text carefully — this guy rises from the third kingdom (Greece), while the guy in chapter 7 appears from the fourth kingdom (Rome) — they're not the same, although similar. This little horn comes before the Antichrist and foreshadows him.

> *And it grew great, even to the host of heaven; and it cast down some of the host and of the stars to the ground, and stamped upon them. Yea, he magnified himself even to the prince of the host, and by him the daily sacrifice was taken away, and the place of his sanctuary was cast down.* Daniel 8:10–11

Antiochus Epiphanes ruled from 175 to 164 BC. His desire was to eliminate the Jews (not a new idea, and one which persists today), or at the least, harass them. 1 Maccabees records the historical account — not inspired, but useful for historical reasons.

> *Moreover king Antiochus wrote to his whole kingdom, that all should be one people, and every one should leave his laws, so all the heathen agreed according to the commandment of the king. Yea, many also of the Israelites consented to his religion, and sacrificed unto idols, and profaned the sabbath. For the king had sent letters by messengers unto Jerusalem and the cities of Judea that they should follow the strange laws of the land, and forbid burnt offerings, and sacrifice, and drink offerings, in the temple; and that they should profane the Sabbaths and festival days, and pollute the sanctuary and holy people, set up altars, and groves, and chapels of idols, and sacrifice swine's flesh, and unclean beasts. That they should*

> *also leave their children uncircumcised, and make their souls abominable with all manner of uncleanness and profanation, to the end they might forget the law, and change all the ordinances. And whosoever would not do according to the commandment of the king, he said, he should die.*
>
> 1 Maccabees 1:44-50

Antiochus performed the ultimate atrocity to the Jews by sacrificing a pig on the altar; not only did a gentile enter the temple, but he sacrificed an unclean animal desecrating the temple. This event yields the technical term "abomination of desolation" you'll see referred to elsewhere in the Bible. It's a specific event of desecration of the temple. The Jews have enough of it and revolt, cleansing and rededicating the temple (celebrated at Hanukkah).

> *And an host was given him against the daily sacrifice by reason of transgression, and it cast down the truth to the ground; and it continued, and prospered.*
>
> Daniel 8:12

Truth is always the first casualty. Remember the armor of God — the foundation comes from the belt of truth. What characterizes today? Lack of truth. As good becomes bad and definitions shift to make whatever point someone requires, we've lost the absolute reference needed to maintain a steady course. What's shocking isn't the occurrence, but rather it's the end result of a specific plan to eliminate God from society.

Why does evil prosper? That's the question people ask. Why does God allow evil? Daniel answers the question in the following verse.

> *Then I heard one saint speaking, and another saint said unto that certain saint which spake, How long shall be the vision concerning the daily sacrifice, and the transgression of desolation, to give both the sanctuary and the host to be trampled under foot?*
>
> Daniel 8:13

Why do bad things happen? How can a loving God allow such evil in the world and innocent people to suffer? The question remains how long will God allow evil? Until the appointed time. It's God's plan, and since He knows more than we do, we must understand information God chooses not to reveal.

> *And he said unto me, Unto two thousand and three hundred days; then shall the sanctuary be cleansed.*
>
> Daniel 8:14

Several theories exist on what these days represent, none of which provide satisfactory answers, so we'll move on.

> *And it came to pass, when I, even I Daniel, had seen the vision, and sought for the meaning, then, behold, there stood before me one having the appearance of a man. And I heard a man's voice between the banks of Ulai, which called, and said, Gabriel, make this man to understand the vision.*
> Daniel 8:15–16

Who is this? Who orders angels?

> *So he came near where I stood; and when he came, I was afraid, and fell upon my face; but he said unto me, Understand, O son of man; for at the time of the end shall be the vision. Now as he was speaking with me, I was in a deep sleep on my face toward the ground; but he touched me, and set me upright. And he said, Behold, I will make thee know what shall be in the last end of the indignation; for at the time appointed the end shall be.*
> Daniel 8:17–19

The appointed time has been determined — the Bible says much about the time we rapidly approach. If you're left behind after the rapture don't believe the lies which follow; pick up your Bible (or one a Christian nicely left behind for you) and you'll know what events will transpire, as it's all been foretold in prophecy. We don't need to worry over why this or that happens — God has a plan and a reason. Sometimes He lets us in on the secret, sometimes not. Whatever God planned goes beyond what you could dream for or hope, but remember God thinks *eternally* while we think *earthly*, and eternal goals might not align with our earthly desires.

All of us have an appointed time allotted to us; you must make the most of what you've been given as when your number is up (as Daniel would say), that's it. Consider the parable of the talents in Matthew 25 as each servant received resources before the master departs on a trip. Upon his return, he demands an account of how each handled what he'd been given. The servant wasting his talent receives the only scolding from the master. It's important to note each grading was independent of the others — the master didn't demand each produce the same results. No, the measure was *what did you do with what you've been given*. We've all been given gifts and time to use them. What are you doing with it?

> *The ram which thou sawest having two horns are the kings of Media and Persia. And the rough goat is the king of Greece, and the great horn that is between his eyes is the first king.*
> Daniel 8:20-21

In case any doubt remained who these animals represent, the Bible interprets itself. Don't fall for pseudo-scholarship covering a failure to read the text. For example, pseudo-scholarship claims Moses didn't write the first five books, Daniel didn't write Daniel, two Isaiahs wrote the book bearing his name, and so on. But Jesus quotes from the first books, and attributes them to Moses. In John 12:38-40 he quotes both halves of Isaiah, attributing *both* to Isaiah (so much for Deutero-Isaiah "scholarship"). We've discussed the authorship of Daniel and pseudo-scholarship previously.

Don't be deceived by false claims of "scholarship," no matter how many PhDs appear behind the name. You can spend weeks destroying their scholarship, or read the Bible and see what it says. Many times the so-called scholars contradict what God said, so will you believe God or man?

> *Now that being broken, whereas four stood up for it, four kingdoms shall stand up out of the nation, but not in his power.*
> Daniel 8:22

Alexander split the kingdom to four generals, but none controlled all. After that one guy arrives, and now we obtain details of him.

> *And in the latter time of their kingdom, when the transgressors are come to the full, a king of fierce countenance, and understanding dark sentences, shall stand up. And his power shall be mighty, but not by his own power; and he shall destroy wonderfully, and shall prosper, and practice, and shall destroy the mighty and the holy people.*
> Daniel 8:23-24

He's smart and filled with Satanic power.

> *And through his policy also he shall cause deceit to prosper in his hand; and he shall magnify himself in his heart, and by peace shall destroy many; he shall also stand up against the Prince of princes; but he shall be broken without hand.*
> Daniel 8:25

Pride and arrogance — Antiochus' life ended by God. Pride is perhaps the greatest sin, as it caused Satan's downfall (and the fall of many others), and we are particularly susceptible to it. But by peace destroys many. World peace is an admirable goal, but it's not going to happen. In this case it produces a counter-result.

> *About that time came Antiochus with dishonor out of the country of Persia. Then swelling with anger he thought to avenge upon the Jews the disgrace done unto him by those that made him flee. Therefore commanded he his chariotman to drive without ceasing, and to dispatch the journey, the judgment of God now following him. For he had spoken proudly in this sort, that he would come to Jerusalem and make it a common burying place of the Jews. But the Lord Almighty, the God of Israel, smote him with an incurable and invisible plague; or as soon as he had spoken these words, a pain of the bowels that was remediless came upon him, and sore torments of the inner parts; Here therefore, being plagued, he began to leave off his great pride, and to come to the knowledge of himself by the scourge of God, his pain increasing every moment. And when he himself could not abide his own smell, he said these words, It is meet to be subject unto God, and that a man that is mortal should not proudly think of himself if he were God.*
>
> 2 Maccabees 9:1,4–5,11–12

Antiochus' ultimate defeat, and the ultimate fate of any who would oppose God. They might think they're getting by with it, but destruction results (Antiochus is a type of Antichrist). See Revelation 20 with Satan cast into the lake of fire with the beast and false prophet (don't be afraid to peek at the end — the answers are in the back of the book). We may not like the timing, but God's plan is perfect, and the timing is right.

> *And the vision of the evening and the morning which was told is true; wherefore shut thou up the vision; for it shall be for many days.*
>
> Daniel 8:26

Many believe in a dual fulfillment for this passage — Antiochus fulfilled it as a type of the coming Antichrist, and much of the vision applies to both.

> *And I Daniel fainted, and was sick certain days; afterward I rose up, and did the king's business; and I was astonished at the vision, but none understood it.*
>
> Daniel 8:27

# Chapter Eight

The physical manifestation of the spiritual into the earthly realm. Don't make the mistake this four-dimensional world we inhabit is the "real" world; Peter tells us this world ends in destruction by fire, while the spiritual world remains. In a few places in the Bible we're given a glimpse into the spiritual dimension, and it's important to realize the spiritual world isn't "out there" somewhere, it surrounds us in dimensions we can't directly experience (see 2 Kings 6 with Elisha and his servant).

*Chapter 10*

# Seventy Weeks of Daniel

THE FAMOUS 70 WEEKS OF Daniel. Even people knowing nothing else of the book have heard of this passage. It's vital to understand this section before you arrive at Revelation or you'll be completely lost; Matthew underscores the importance of the prophecy as it's *specifically* called out for understanding.

> *When ye therefore shall see the abomination of desolation, spoken of by Daniel the prophet, stand in the holy place,* (**whoso readeth, let him understand**)   Matt 24:15

Consider the verses in context, as they form the framework to understand all prophecy.

> *Seventy weeks are determined upon thy people and upon thy holy city, to finish the transgression, and to make an end of sins, and to make reconciliation for iniquity, and to bring in everlasting righteousness, and to seal up the vision and prophecy, and to anoint the most Holy. Know therefore and understand, that from the going forth of the commandment to restore and to build Jerusalem unto the Messiah the Prince shall be seven weeks, and threescore and two weeks; the street shall be built again, and the wall, even in troublous times. And after threescore and two weeks shall Messiah be cut off, but not for himself; and the people of the prince that shall come shall destroy the city and the sanctuary; and the end thereof shall be with a flood, and unto the end of the war desolations are determined. And he shall confirm the covenant with many for one week; and in the midst of the week he shall cause the sacrifice and*

*the oblation to cease, and for the overspreading of abominations he shall make it desolate, even until the consummation, and that determined shall be poured upon the desolate.*

Daniel 9:24–27

Note the implicit technology — when you see. We immediately take that for granted, but prior to satellite TV and Internet, only a few could see the Holy Place at once, while these events will be viewable worldwide. It's only recently (since the 1970s or so) where technology existed for the world to watch events unfold live.

A few notes to avoid bad information, and should be obvious from even a casual reading (though surprisingly many miss):

- It's about the Jews, *not* the church. It's Daniel's people (the Jews) and their Holy City (Jerusalem).
- It hasn't happened yet. The end of sin, everlasting righteousness, and so on. Some attempt to claim a previous fulfillment, but then the news must have skipped reporting the end of sin and the beginning of everlasting righteousness.
- The seventy weeks are not continuous. A gap appears between the 69$^{th}$ week and the 70$^{th}$ week.
- Revelation details the 70$^{th}$ week (mainly chapters 6–19).

Keeping a few facts in mind avoids pitfalls and places you ahead of scholars who don't read the book. You'll notice God deals with the church and Jews separately. Before Jesus, God dealt with the Jews (Gentiles were only included if they became a Jew). Since Jesus' death and resurrection, God dealt with the Gentiles. This leads some to believe God abandoned the Jews, and their promises are now bestowed on the church.

Nonsense — God's promises to Abraham in Genesis are unconditional and irrevocable; the Jewish people still have a destiny to be fulfilled. Don't believe the Jews aren't important anymore, or God's promises to them have now fallen on the church.

We'll break the prophecy down into a few sections:

- v24 — Overview.
- v25 — The sixty-nine weeks (complete).
- v26a — The Messiah.
- v26b — The interval between week sixty-nine and seventy (where we're currently at).
- v27 — The final week (still future, but detailed in Revelation).

## The Overview

> *Seventy weeks are determined upon thy people and upon thy holy city, to finish the transgression, and to make an end of sins, and to make reconciliation for iniquity, and to bring in everlasting righteousness, and to seal up the vision and prophecy, and to anoint the most Holy.* Daniel 9:24

As noted, it's obvious this prophecy concerns the Jews and the city of Jerusalem, not the Church. Second, while history records the fulfillment of parts of the prophecy, parts remain future. Obviously, an end of sin hasn't occurred, nor everlasting righteousness.

What are the seventy weeks? The Hebrew says seventy sevens, and it's translated weeks. Similar to our use of decade (meaning ten years), in this context the Hebrew clearly implies a week means seven years. One note; Bible prophecy uses 360 day years. Why isn't important, but if calculating this yourself you can't use the current 365-day calendar.

It does represent a literal period — it's not an allegory and must be understood to be literal. To jump ahead a bit, several allusions to the 70$^{th}$ week appear elsewhere in the Bible, each describing the time a bit differently, yet equally.

- 42 months — Revelation 11:2, 13:5
- 1,260 days — Revelation 11:3, 12:6
- Half of one week (literally "sevens") — Daniel 9:27
- Times, time and half a time (3 ½ years) — Daniel 12:7

Notice 1260 divided by 3.5 = 360 — a year in the Bible equals 360 days. Chuck Missler notes ancient calendars changed around 700 BC from 360 days to the current 365 ¼ days, although each did differently. Why the change occurred might be historically interesting, but not important here, and left as an exercise for the interested reader.

## The 69 Weeks

> *Know therefore and understand, that from the going forth of the commandment to restore and to build Jerusalem unto the Messiah the Prince shall be seven weeks, and threescore and two weeks; the street shall be built again, and the wall, even in troublous times.* Daniel 9:25

For most of this discussion, we're going to use Sir Robert Anderson's work "The Coming Prince," cited by Chuck Missler, J Vernon McGee, and most other scholars (no we didn't do all this work ourselves).

Notice it's a prediction, with a starting event, mathematical number, and a terminating event. This should be easy to verify or disprove for critics. It's the exact nature of this prophecy (and others in Daniel) leading skeptics to late date the book by a pen other than Daniel's. The research exists on shaky ground, but the presumption is God doesn't exist, therefore prophecy doesn't exist, thus it's impossible for Daniel to have known the future with such precision.

Daniel's error is zero. Compare to the prophets you'll find in the National Enquirer (or political or economic pundits) who receive great accolades if they get it *half* right. Bible prophets maintain 100% accuracy, and would be stoned if something uttered failed to come true — the yardstick for prophets of God is 100% accuracy, all the time.

> *But the prophet, which shall presume to speak a word in my name, which I have not commanded him to speak, or that shall speak in the name of other gods, even that prophet shall die. And if thou say in thine heart, How shall we know the word which the LORD hath not spoken? When a prophet speaketh in the name of the LORD, if the thing follow not, nor come to pass, that is the thing which the LORD hath not spoken, but the prophet hath spoken it presumptuously; thou shalt not be afraid of him.*     Deuteronomy 18:20–22

Let's break down the sixty-nine weeks for further analysis:

- START: from the going forth of the command to restore and build Jerusalem.
- NUMBER: There shall be seven weeks and sixty-two weeks.
- FINAL EVENT: Until Messiah the Prince.

When did this start? Perhaps your Bible mentions three possibilities for this event (actually four).

- Cyrus in Ezra 1:1–4 (First year of Cyrus)
- Darius in Ezra 6:1–12 (First year of Darius)
- Artaxerxes in Ezra 7:11–26 (Seventh year Artaxerxes)
- Artaxerxes in Nehemiah 2:1–8 (Twentieth year Artaxerxes)

# Seventy Weeks of Daniel

So which is it? Return to the text to discover one more clue "The street shall be built again, and the wall, even in troublous times." Only Nehemiah mentions the wall, with the decree occurring in 445 BC in the month of Nisan. Notice how simple Bible prophecy becomes when you just take what it says as what it means? Imagine all the problems we'd have if we tried to allegorize it. Accept it as it says and you'll be fine.

Mark Eastman in his book "The Search for Messiah" states it's Hebrew tradition when the day of month isn't mentioned specifically it means the first day*. According to Nehemiah, the starting point is the first of Nisan in the twentieth year of Artaxerxes. The interval is easy as 69 weeks of 360 day years is 173,880 days. What's the final event? Until the coming of the Jewish Messiah. And that's the whole prophecy.

If you do the calendar work, moving forward from Nisan 445 BC 173,880 days you'll arrive at the tenth of Nisan 32 AD [†], known as April 6, 32 AD. So What? The significance comes from Jesus himself, after the events of what we call Palm Sunday, as He weeps over the city.

> *And when he was come near, he beheld the city, and wept over it, Saying, If thou hadst known, even thou, at least in this thy day, the things which belong unto thy peace! But now they are hid from thine eyes. For the days shall come upon thee, that thine enemies shall cast a trench about thee, and compass thee round, and keep thee in on every side, And shall lay thee even with the ground, and thy children within thee; and they shall not leave in thee one stone upon another; because thou knewest not the time of thy visitation.*     Luke 19:41–44

As you read the Gospels, you'll notice a few times the crowd tries to make Him king, but He slips away, saying My time has not yet come. On this specific day, He not only allowed it, He arranged it. Why? It's the exact day from the prophecy in Daniel.

Jesus held them accountable to know. The prophecy isn't hard to understand, and if we can figure out the events thousands of years later, the Jews certainly should have understood. It's not allegorical or theoretical; the creator of the universe holds people accountable to what He's said. Something else must explain why the Jews missed it.

---

\*     http://blueletterbible.org/Comm/mark_eastman/messiah/sfm_06.html
[†]    McGee (1982, page 588)

> *The scepter shall not depart from Judah, nor a lawgiver from between his feet, until Shiloh come; and unto him shall the gathering of the people be.*   Genesis 49:10

To distill the verse, it means the Jews would not have capital punishment taken away from them until the Messiah appears. As Rome takes over Israel, the Jewish leaders lament, for they think the scripture has been broken. Yet they did not know about a young boy growing up among them in a local town; the Jewish leaders believed God's Word had been broken.

They imposed presuppositions to the text, and possibly for that, missed their Messiah. Don't do that. Don't force your ideas on the Bible. God sometimes does things a little strange, at least the way we see it. But the prophecy is clear — "Surely the Lord GOD will do nothing, but he revealeth his secret unto his servants the prophets" (Amos 3:7).

Okay, you're a skeptic. Consider another way, as Mark Eastman* notes the following. Luke chapter 3 states Jesus' baptism occurs in the fifteenth year of Tiberius. Tiberius's reign began on August 19 14 AD, so Jesus' first Passover would have been spring AD 29. Most believe Jesus' ministry was 3 ½ years, so the fourth would have been 32 AD. And in 32 AD, the Sunday before Passover that year was April 6, 32 AD, the same day given to Daniel (what a coincidence!).

So that's verse 25. So far it's been simple. But once you arrive, what happens?

### The Messiah

> *And after threescore and two weeks shall Messiah be cut off, but not for himself*   Daniel 9:26a

After sixty-two weeks is the same as after the sixty-nine weeks (as it's 7 + 62). After that period the Messiah shall be cut off (which means executed). But not for Himself (substitution); of course Jesus Himself was innocent, He paid the price for *my* sin, not His (He was sinless), as Chuck Missler examines the gospel according to Barabbas: †

> *The substitution of Barabbas over Jesus before Pilate on that fateful day has profound implications for each of us. It is il-*

---
\*   http://blueletterbible.org/Comm/mark_eastman/messiah/sfm_06.html
†   http://www.khouse.org/articles/2000/217/

*luminating to examine the contrast between the two accused more closely:*

- *Barabbas stood under the righteous condemnation of the law.*
- *Barabbas knew the One who was to take his cross and take his place was innocent.*
- *Barabbas knew that Jesus Christ was for him a true substitute.*
- *Barabbas knew that he had done nothing to merit going free while another took his place.*
- *Barabbas knew Christ's death was for him perfectly efficacious.*
- *Barabbas and Jesus changed places! "The murderer's bonds, curse, disgrace, and mortal agony were transferred to the righteous Jesus; while the liberty, innocence, safety, and well-being of the immaculate Nazarene became the lot of the murderer.*

## The Interval

*and the people of the prince that shall come shall destroy the city and the sanctuary; and the end thereof shall be with a flood, and unto the end of the war desolations are determined.*
Daniel 9:26b

How do we know an interval exists between 69th and 70th week? Carefully read the passage again, "the people of the prince who is to come shall destroy the city and the sanctuary." The prince who is to come refers to Antichrist, and his people (the Romans) destroyed Jerusalem in 70 AD as a historical event. We know by history the interval lasts at least from 32 AD to 70 AD, and by real experience it's been over 2,000 years.

But the 70th week draws near.

Back to what we started with, this passage concerns the Jews, not the church. What happens in the 70th week? You'll discover in Revelation chapters 6–19, but notice what Daniel says regarding the 70th week.

## The 70th Week

*And he shall confirm the covenant with many for one week; and in the midst of the week he shall cause the sacrifice and the oblation to cease, and for the overspreading of abominations he*

> *shall make it desolate, even until the consummation, and that determined shall be poured upon the desolate.*   Daniel 9:27

He is "the prince who is to come," the Antichrist. He shall enforce an agreement with Israel (whether he makes the agreement itself is debatable), but in the middle of the period he breaks the covenant, committing the abomination which causes desolation — it's then the Jews realize their mistake; Revelation expands on the 70$^{th}$ week if you're interested.

## Conclusion

History records the fulfillment of the first sixty-nine weeks perfectly, do you have any doubt the 70$^{th}$ week will be? This passage poses no problems if you take it as it reads, and not try to allegorize it. The events are sure — but where is the United States in the end times? It's not mentioned much in the Bible. Why not?

Society continues to degrade — Robert Bork wrote a book called "Slouching toward Gomorrah"; the provocative title prophetic as we head toward value relativism and moral relativism, losing the moral absolutes of God's Word in all corners of society. Schools fail to teach basic logic and analysis skills, turning out people ignorant of basic skills making them easy pickings for anyone desiring to subvert the truth. We're rapidly slouching back toward the time of Judges, where "everyone did what was right in their own eyes," and moral absolutes become lost in a sea of relativism, the dive rate into the depths increasing at the dawn of the pandemic age (2019–2021) which found the church dividing over more useless garbage instead of ministering to a world desperately needing it.

Some say the situation is hopeless, yet Nineveh was forty days from destruction and turned around. Since the United States isn't in prophecy we don't know the end; it's possible to change course (if the church and its pastors can get their act together). The problem does not lie with Congress or president, it's us; the politicians are *our* employees, *we* put them in office, and by our votes we can remove them (more on that in chapter 9).

> *If my people, which are called by my name, shall humble themselves, and pray, and seek my face, and turn from their wicked ways; then will I hear from heaven, and will forgive their sin, and will heal their land.*   2 Chronicles 7:14

We will be held accountable as stewards for the republic; we hired the guys leading the country and the pastors leading our fellowships. If they be Godly, moral men, it's because we demand it be so. Some Christians don't like to be involved or (gasp!) calling a pastor on the carpet for bizarre detours into church-irrelevant issues like politics, yet as a steward you *must* be. Allowing politicians or pastors to run amok won't be healthy from either a country viewpoint, or a church one.

*And of the children of Issachar, who were men that had understanding of the times, to know what Israel ought to do;*
1 Chronicles 12:32

*Chapter 11*

# Chapter Nine

THE DAYTONA 500 RACE EACH February provides a reminder NASCAR remains one sport prayer continues to occur before the event, even if those prayers are general and politically correct. Similar prayers occur before legislatures convene, but what if someone didn't read the memo regarding politically correct content? You'd get pastor Joe Wright — January 1996 in Kansas.[*] Different wordings of the text exist[†], although the basic concept remains the same.

> *Heavenly Father, we come before you to ask your forgiveness. We seek your direction and your guidance. We know your word says, "Woe to those who call evil good." But that's what we've done.*
>
> *We've lost our spiritual equilibrium. We have inverted our values. We have ridiculed the absolute truth of your word in the name of moral pluralism. We have worshiped other gods and called it multiculturalism. We have endorsed perversion and called it an alternative lifestyle. We've exploited the poor and called it a lottery. We've neglected the needy and called it self-preservation. We have rewarded laziness and called it welfare. In the name of choice, we have killed our unborn. In the name of right to life, we have killed abortionists.*

---

[*] Fisher (1996)
[†] We've never found a *definitive* version of the text. It's been reported on by many people over the years, but a singular authoritative source doesn't appear to exist. As the event occurred pre-Internet age (1996), that's not unexpected.

*We have neglected to discipline our children and called it building self-esteem. We have abused power and called it political savvy. We have coveted our neighbor's possessions and called it taxes. We have polluted the air with profanity and pornography and called it freedom of expression. We have ridiculed the time-honored values of our forefathers and called it enlightenment.*

*Search us, oh, God, and know our hearts today. Try us. Show us any wickedness within us. Cleanse us from every sin and set us free. Guide and bless these men and women who have been sent here by the people of the State of Kansas, and that they have been ordained by you to govern this great state.*

*Grant them your wisdom to rule. May their decisions direct us to the center of your will. And, as we continue our prayer and as we come in out of the fog, give us clear minds to accomplish our goals as we begin this Legislature. For we pray in Jesus' name, Amen.*

Whoops — while it represents a 1996-centric mentality and textual representation, compare Pastor Wright's prayer with Daniel's prayer in chapter 9 as they both involve sins of the people, both name specific sins they're guilty of, and both use "we" and include themselves in the problem.

So we've evolved, right? Perhaps not much — the prayers display similar characteristics as our society continues to deviate from God's law, and the government moves more and more to censor God — Daniel 9 sounds like anything we could pray about our country (there's a lesson in there somewhere).

We're heading toward value relativism and moral relativism, as atheism becomes the official state religion in opposition to the freedom of religion the country was founded on, but that's another topic (it's freedom *to*, not freedom *from*). Everybody does what is right in their own eyes, and tolerance doesn't mean allowing everyone freedom to worship what and how they want, tolerance means *no absolutes exist*, and anyone claiming so displays intolerance and must be silenced (Doublespeak at its best; Orwell would be proud).

The ultimate irony comes from the only remaining absolute — *there are no absolutes*, which makes as much sense as the Cretan saying "all Cretians are liars (Titus 1:12)". No absolute moral authority exists; each person acts according to whatever works for their perception of morality, and society de-evolves back to Judges as "everyone does what was right in their own eyes." Sound familiar? We don't want to restrict anybody from anything anymore. Value relativism, situational ethics, and 1984-esqe redefinitions of words (George Orwell would be proud, if just a few years late on his predictions) — without God, anything is possible (Bill Ritchie).

Worse, those philosophies infest the church, as its leaders proclaim value relativism replaces the Bible. Oh, they won't *say* it that way, but when they exhibit and promote lawlessness (ignore rules you don't like, and deception is okay as the end justifies the means) it's the church aligning itself with the fruit of the flesh instead of the fruit of the spirit.

Nineveh was forty days from destruction — it's possible to turn it around as God does perform miracles (I believe Billy Graham said if God doesn't judge America for her sins, he'll have to apologize to Sodom and Gomorrah). As value relativism continues to seep across the country like a toxic waste spill, the country loses its moral compass and the sense of right and wrong. If it feels good, do it.

*If my people, which are called by my name, shall humble themselves, and pray, and seek my face, and turn from their wicked ways; then will I hear from heaven, and will forgive their sin, and will heal their land.* 2 Chronicles 7:14

We will be held accountable as stewards; we hired the guys leading the county and our churches. If they be Godly men and men of integrity, it's because the people demand it. If they be men without morals and choose to promote sin, it's because the people allow it. Corrupt leaders display symptoms of the problem — the attempt to exterminate God and His Word from all corners of society (even in the church).

After the elimination of God, no absolutes remain and it's a moral free for all (and free-fall); it's back to the times of the Judges (read the book and see what happens when a society becomes a moral free-for-all without the absolute standard of God's Word).

Many Christians don't want to be involved, yet it's required of stewards to be faithful (1 Corinthians 4:2). Are you afraid to get involved in your child's life (we hope not)? Then why be afraid of politics or standing up against corrupt church leaders? Compare Daniel's prayer to today as Daniel involved himself in politics, but not by carrying a sign or protesting (the solution isn't to be found in PAC's). What did he do? He took a stand, and supported biblical principles. Everything passed through the filter of God's Word. If it passes the test, it's acceptable, if not, it isn't.

We're not discussing waving signs and protesting or shouting vote for this guy or passing out voter education guides, but a simple idea: find out what candidates and pastors believe and support those holding biblical principles. We can all agree on that. It's not supporting one political party or denomination over another, but supporting people who hold true to Biblical principles.

Too many pastors trade politics for ministry. This does *not* mean *individual* Christians should not be politically active, but dragging the church through the mud of political issues will always be stunningly stupid as pastors abandon the primary mission and focus of the church to focus on minor irrelevant ideas — focusing on differences to create disunity, division, and chaos instead of ministering. The church holds a long history of division over foolish, trivial, and irrelevant items — pre-trib, Calvinism, Bible translations, baptism, and more.

The dawn of the pandemic age (2019–2021) proved again how low the church and its pastors can stoop, as if the old dumb divisions weren't enough, pastors of the pandemic age created *new* ones, instead of repairing old ones. The cure? Simple. Avoid stupid disputes and division over petty non-doctrinal issues and return to the Gospel ... at least as Paul defines it.

> *I passed on to you what was most important and what had also been passed on to me. Christ died for our sins, just as the Scriptures said. He was buried, and he was raised from the dead on the third day, just as the Scriptures said.*
>
> 1 Corinthians 15:3—4 NLT

The Gospel. Pastors in the pandemic age forgot it to focus on politics and division. It will be a great mystery for the ages why church leaders enjoy creating division, discovering new ways to degrade members instead of building them up.

- You've been divorced dear, sorry, you can't fellowship here.
- You voted for candidate X? Sorry, disallowed.
- Calvinism? Nope, you're excluded (or included).
- Pandemic era health protections? Be gone.

The church and its leaders fail to comprehend their mission. Church leaders continuing to divide over anything *not* the Gospel remains something they'll need to answer for, as Jesus told the Pharisees (and think about today's Pharisees acting similarly).

> *What sorrow awaits you teachers of religious law and you Pharisees. Hypocrites! For you cross land and sea to make one convert, and then you turn that person into twice the child of hell you yourselves are!* Matthew 23:15 NLT

A pastor who can stand up Sunday and say "we're glad you're here, we want to spread the love of God" and on Monday divide the fellowship into groups based on his personal political (not doctrinal) opinions, *or* trivial doctrine (baptism) has some 'splaining to do.

If churches return to focusing on the Gospel and not worry or divide over petty doctrinal issues (or politics), the church would be much stronger. Sadly, church history shows pandemic-age pastors prove another example of how church leadership drives off course. *The* Gospel is as Paul defines. Period. The church and its leaders would be wise to follow Paul's teaching.

While those pastors errored wildly off course into the ditch, members failing to be involved also err. We *will* be held accountable for our stewardship of the country and the church. If our leadership be Godly, it's because people demand it. If they slouch toward Gomorrah, it's because people tolerate it. You're a steward of your vote; do homework and exercise your stewardship wisely.

> *In the first year of Darius the son of Ahasuerus, of the seed of the Medes, which was made king over the realm of the Chaldeans; In the first year of his reign I Daniel understood by books the number of the years, whereof the word of the LORD came to Jeremiah the prophet, that he would accomplish seventy years in the desolations of Jerusalem.* Daniel 9:1-2

Why are they in captivity in the first place? They ignored God's law; nations ignore God's law at their own peril. God may *allow* transgression for a period of time, but that does not mean He *approves* of it. At some point, judgment comes. For Israel, they ignored the Sabbath for the land and eventually God judged them for it.

> *Moreover all the chief of the priests, and the people, transgressed very much after all the abominations of the nations; and polluted the house of the LORD which he had hallowed in Jerusalem. And the LORD God of their fathers sent to them*

> *by his messengers, rising up early, and sending, because he had compassion on his people, and on his dwelling place; But they mocked the messengers of God, and despised his words, and misused his prophets, until the wrath of the LORD arose against his people, till there was no remedy. ... To fulfill the word of the LORD by the mouth of Jeremiah, until the land had enjoyed her Sabbaths; for as long as she lay desolate she kept sabbath, to fulfill threescore and ten years.*
>
> 2 Chronicles 36:14-16, 21

As the Sabbath week existed for man, a Sabbath year for the land existed as well. The land was worked six years, and allowed to rest on the seventh. Israel ignored it so long the Lord says the land must rest for its Sabbaths, and thus the captivity involving Daniel begins.

They had warning — God sent messengers which they ignored. Sound familiar? People mock and despise men of God as nobody wants to hear the warnings. But judgment will come. Nevertheless, as the longsuffering and patience of God allows time for repentance, at some point enough is enough and judgment comes.

Daniel understands the fulfillment of Jeremiah in 25:11-12 & 29:10 draws near; about 67 of the 70 years passed as Daniel begins his prayer. Daniel took Jeremiah's prophecy literally with no attempt to allegorize it. An important concept when you study Revelation — take it as it says. When it says one-third of the grass burns up it means exactly that. Revelation isn't hard because we don't understand it, but because we do and don't like what it says.

> *And I set my face unto the Lord God, to seek by prayer and supplication, with fasting, and sackcloth, and ashes.*
>
> Daniel 9:3

Daniel prays for what he knows will happen. It's a short and not long-winded prayer, but covers important points. First, he starts with the right attitude and humility. You can't go to the God of the universe with arrogance and pride, but neither can you go with timidity and fear. As always, you need balance.

> *Let us therefore come boldly unto the throne of grace, that we may obtain mercy, and find grace to help in time of need.*
>
> Hebrews 4:16

Surely God doesn't want to be bothered? What does Paul say?

# Chapter Nine

*Be anxious for nothing; but in everything by prayer and supplication with thanksgiving let your requests be made known unto God.*                                 Philippians 4:6

Yeah, but what does everything mean? It means the big stuff right? Au contraire.

*In the beginning was the Word, and the Word was with God, and the Word was God. The same was in the beginning with God. All things were made by him; and without him was not any thing made that was made.*              John 1:1-3

All things were made by Him and nothing was made without Him; the same Greek appears in John as Paul used in Philippians. All means all — even the little stuff. God wants to hear from you. You're not bugging God, all things means all things. Understand who you're talking to, but don't be afraid — He *wants* to hear from you in all things — and all means all, that's all all means.

*And I prayed unto the LORD my God, and made my confession, and said, O Lord, the great and awesome God, keeping the covenant and mercy to them that love him, and to them that keep his commandments;*              Daniel 9:4

Note why he's praying — he knows the captivity draws to a conclusion, but doesn't mention it yet as he confesses sin first. A misnomer exists over confessing sin — it's not a catholic idea with a priest and absolution, it's agreeing with God the sin exists.

He begins with a statement of who God is. Two errors must be avoided in your approach to God — too casual and too formal. He's not the "man upstairs," but neither should you be afraid of Him. It's neither "yo God" nor "Thou O Lord," and King James English doesn't make your prayer heard faster. Consider examples of both with Moses.

- Exodus 3 — Moses and the burning bush as God says take off your shoes, you're standing on holy ground. Approaching God with the proper attitude of respect and reverence.
- Exodus 20 — God gives Moses the ten commandments. The people (verse 18) are fearful and only want Moses to speak to them. That's improper fear and timidity.

Maintain balance as Satan attempts driving you off to either side. He doesn't believe anything except to drive you away from truth. Neither casual nor fear is correct; approach God with proper respect, but don't fail to include Him in *all* things.

> *We have sinned, and have committed iniquity, and have done wickedly, and have rebelled, even by departing from thy precepts and from thine ordinances:* Daniel 9:5

Daniel states facts; he doesn't try to rationalize away sin. Chuck Missler says never underestimate a human's ability to rationalize, and once you understand you'll be amazed at how often you see it. Sin is sin. Period.

Daniel includes himself — "*we* have sinned." He cites specific examples (wickedness, rebellion, ignoring God's law). All have sinned and fallen short of the glory of God (Romans 3:23). The Greek in John 1:3, Philippians 4:6 and Romans 3:23 contains the same word. All means all, that's all all means. Your situation isn't different — sin is still sin. Don't try and rationalize it.

> *Neither have we hearkened unto thy servants the prophets, which spoke in thy name to our kings, our princes, and our fathers, and to all the people of the land. O Lord, righteousness belongeth unto thee, but unto us confusion of faces, as at this day; to the men of Judah, and to the inhabitants of Jerusalem, and unto all Israel, that are near, and that are far off, through all the countries to which thou hast driven them, because of their trespass that they have trespassed against thee.* Daniel 9:6–7

Not only did they fall away from the law, they ignored the people sent by God to warn them. Sound familiar? Wickedness, rebellion against God, ignoring His law, and refusing to heed the warning from men God sent. Has man evolved since Daniel's time? It doesn't appear so. The only thing man learns from history is man learns nothing from history — mistakes repeat again and again.

People don't like to hear truth, ignoring, rationalizing it away, or finding people who tell them what they want to hear. It's normal to rationalize your situation — after all, it's different (NOT!). Sin is sin, and we're all guilty before God. People turn away from truth toward others who speak not the truth, but what they want to hear.

> *For the time will come when they will not endure sound doctrine; but after their own lusts shall they heap to themselves teachers, having itching ears; And they shall turn away their*

*ears from the truth, and shall be turned unto fables.*
2 Timothy 4:3–4

God's rules apply to everyone, all the time, in every situation. You must speak the truth in love — not sandwich-board evangelism. If people reject it, fine; it's not your job to be the Holy Spirit, only to provide information. The responsibility for that knowledge falls on the individual person.

*O Lord, to us belongeth confusion of face, to our kings, to our princes, and to our fathers, because we have sinned against thee. To the Lord our God belong mercies and forgivenesses, though we have rebelled against him;*  Daniel 9:8–9

It's our fault, not the Twinkies.* It's popular today to blame everyone else *but* the person responsible. It's not your fault, you have a disease. Where is personal responsibility? To paraphrase for modern times, to *us* belongs shame, our President, our congress and our fathers have sinned against you.

Remember "the buck stops here"? Today it's pass the buck as nobody claims responsibility for anything (Chutzpah is murdering your parents and throwing yourself on the mercy of the court because you're an orphan.† What does Daniel say — we have sinned against you. It's *our* fault. We're responsible. He's lived in captivity for decades, and could easily pass the buck (it's not my fault we're here, I was just a kid) — but doesn't.

*Neither have we obeyed the voice of the LORD our God, to walk in his laws, which he set before us by his servants the prophets. Yea, all Israel have transgressed thy law, even by departing, that they might not obey thy voice; therefore the curse is poured upon us, and the oath that is written in the law of Moses the servant of God, because we have sinned against him.*
Daniel 9:10–11

God made His law clear. Some things are bad — don't do them or promote them. Today it's popular to say the Bible needs to

---
\*  The 1979 trial of Dan White, who murdered the San Francisco mayor and a supervisor. At trial, it was argued he was depressed and became more depressed due to high sugar intake of Twinkies and soda. The conviction of manslaughter instead of first-degree murder could be credited to the Twinkie defense. And a legend was born.

†  It's likely a Chuck Missler quote, but any specific reference to the actual author is difficult to find.

change with society and doesn't apply to modern life or certain situations. But *if* God exists, can't He design a message for all generations and situations? I think so. The Bible doesn't change. God's law is God's law. You don't have to follow it if you don't want, but you can't change what God says. As a nation, have we abandoned God's law? Let the reader decide for themselves if the words of Daniel's prayer apply equally today.

> *Behold, I set before you this day a blessing and a curse; A blessing, if ye obey the commandments of the LORD your God, which I command you this day; And a curse, if ye will not obey the commandments of the LORD your God, but turn aside out of the way which I command you this day, to go after other gods, which ye have not known.* Deuteronomy 11:26-28

God doesn't force you into anything — it's your choice, it's the choice facing the country. Some may say, we haven't served other gods, have we? Perhaps not the idol, but the old pagan gods remain, waiting to ensnare you.

- Ashtoreth — Pleasure and sexuality.
- Baal — Power.
- Mammon — Money.
- Molech — Practicality. Molech's statue had arms outstretched and they built a fire in his belly until he glowed red-hot; if you sacrificed your first child Molech honors your sacrifice and blessed you. It was *practical* to sacrifice one to be blessed.
- Nebo — God of knowledge and wisdom.

Old pagan gods exist today, perhaps not as statues, but they're worshiped nonetheless. As Israel at times fell into idolatry, Christians must be careful as many worship ancient gods — just because an idol doesn't exist doesn't mean these gods aren't still around. Through all this, Daniel hasn't mentioned his petition yet!

> *And he hath confirmed his words, which he spoke against us, and against our judges that judged us, by bringing upon us a great evil; for under the whole heaven hath not been done as hath been done upon Jerusalem. As it is written in the law of Moses, all this evil is come upon us; yet made we not our prayer before the LORD our God, that we might turn from our iniquities, and understand thy truth.* Daniel 9:12-13

God warned them, the nation ignored, and judgment came. Even after judgment they ignored God, an example of stiff-necked and refusing to yield no matter what. The same attitude exists in Revelation as the people refuse to repent as well. For the United States, we've been warned, how long will God's mercy last when we openly flaunt rebellion against God? When the promotion of sin becomes top priority? How long? Nobody knows, but the relevance of Daniel's prayer remains today.

> *Therefore hath the LORD watched upon the evil, and brought it upon us; for the LORD our God is righteous in all his works which he doeth; for we obeyed not his voice. And now, O Lord our God, that hast brought thy people forth out of the land of Egypt with a mighty hand, and hast gotten thee renown, as at this day; we have sinned, we have done wickedly.*
> Daniel 9:14-15

Daniel admits they got what they deserved; the wages of sin is death; since all sin, all deserve death. No attempt to rationalize appears anywhere in Daniel's prayer as Daniel speaks the truth, straight out. He's acknowledged God and confessed his sin, so now he can petition God.

> *O Lord, according to all thy righteousness, I beseech thee, let thine anger and thy fury be turned away from thy city Jerusalem, thy holy mountain; because for our sins, and for the iniquities of our fathers, Jerusalem and thy people are become a reproach to all that are about us. Now therefore, O our God, hear the prayer of thy servant, and his supplications, and cause thy face to shine upon thy sanctuary that is desolate, for the Lord's sake.*
> Daniel 9:16-17

Daniel doesn't ask because Israel is good, but because the Lord is. Daniel knows they deserve punishment for their sin, but wants mercy. Don't pray for justice, but mercy.

> *O my God, incline thine ear, and hear; open thine eyes, and behold our desolations, and the city which is called by thy name; for we do not present our supplications before thee for our righteousnesses, but for thy great mercies. O Lord, hear; O Lord, forgive; O Lord, hearken and do; defer not, for thine own sake, O my God; for thy city and thy people are called by thy name.*
> Daniel 9:18-19

The deliverance does not come because of what they did, but because of God's promises; the basis for the request isn't on what he's done, but on God's character as mercy is not getting what you deserve. In the case of sin, death. As a nation, destruction.

> *And while I was speaking, and praying, and confessing my sin and the sin of my people Israel, and presenting my supplication before the LORD my God for the holy mountain of my God; Yea, while I was speaking in prayer, even the man Gabriel, whom I had seen in the vision at the beginning, being caused to fly swiftly, touched me about the time of the evening oblation.*
> Daniel 9:20–21

During the prayer an angel interrupts him about the time of the evening offering. Daniel lived in captivity for decades, yet continues measuring time by temple sacrifices, showing where his heart is. Character matters.

> *And he informed me, and talked with me, and said, O Daniel, I am now come forth to give thee skill and understanding. At the beginning of thy supplications the commandment came forth, and I am come to show thee; for thou art greatly beloved; therefore understand the matter, and consider the vision.*
> Daniel 9:22–23

The famous seventy weeks of Daniel, which we've covered in a section by itself.

> *Seventy weeks are determined upon thy people and upon thy holy city, to finish the transgression, and to make an end of sins, and to make reconciliation for iniquity, and to bring in everlasting righteousness, and to seal up the vision and prophecy, and to anoint the most Holy. Know therefore and understand, that from the going forth of the commandment to restore and to build Jerusalem unto the Messiah the Prince shall be seven weeks, and threescore and two weeks; the street shall be built again, and the wall, even in troublous times. And after threescore and two weeks shall Messiah be cut off, but not for himself; and the people of the prince that shall come shall destroy the city and the sanctuary; and the end thereof shall be with a flood, and unto the end of the war desolations are determined. And he shall confirm the covenant with many for one week; and in the midst of the week he shall cause the sacrifice and*

> *the oblation to cease, and for the overspreading of abominations he shall make it desolate, even until the consummation, and that determined shall be poured upon the desolate.*
> Daniel 9:24–27

Daniel's prayer for his country was a modern one. Does the idea in Judges "everyone did what was right in their own eyes" sound familiar? We don't want to restrict anybody from anything anymore. Value relativism, situational ethics, do whatever feels right for you — without God, anything is possible.

> *If my people, which are called by my name, shall humble themselves, and pray, and seek my face, and turn from their wicked ways; then will I hear from heaven, and will forgive their sin, and will heal their land.*
> 2 Chronicles 7:14

That's a description of Daniel 9. We will be held accountable as stewards, we hired the guys posing as leaders (both in government and the church). If they be Godly, it's because people demand it. If they be ungodly, it's because people allow it.

*Chapter 12*

# Chapter Ten

THE FINAL CHAPTERS OF DANIEL detail one vision. Chapter 10 contains the setup, and 11–12 describe the vision in detail. This section explains why critics attack the book of Daniel as it contains such clear visions of future events (and since God doesn't exist) it's not possible for anyone to predict future events with such accuracy. Of course, the skeptic's bias becomes known as their presupposition of the lack of God becomes an assumption they must make for their theory to be true.

> *In the third year of Cyrus king of Persia a thing was revealed unto Daniel, whose name was called Belteshazzar; and the thing was true, but the time appointed was long: and he understood the thing, and had understanding of the vision.*
> 
> Daniel 10:1

After living in captivity most of his life, Daniel reaches the age of 85 — long after retirement, he's not beyond the age God can use him. Don't think you're too old, too young, not smart enough or any other disqualifier. God desires a willing heart to serve Him — that's all.

> *In those days I Daniel was mourning three full weeks.*
> 
> Daniel 10:2

Three weeks? That's dedication. He didn't hear an answer, yet continued (we'll see why the answer was delayed soon). Yet another insight into the character of Daniel, and a lesson for us today. It's a common question to ask, how long should I pray for something? The simple answer — until you receive a reply. Remember, no is an answer as well (even if you don't like it).

Daniel mourns for Jerusalem and his people the Jews. The vision arrives in the third year of Cyrus — in Ezra 1:1–4 Cyrus allowed the Jews to return and build the temple, but not many took advantage of the offer. These events occur two years later, with few actually returning (42,360 according to Ezra 2:64) — they preferred the comfort of captivity over engaging the Lord's work.

> *If ye love wealth greater than liberty, the tranquility of servitude greater than the animating contest for freedom, go home from us in peace. We seek not your counsel, nor your arms. Crouch down and lick the hand that feeds you; May your chains set lightly upon you, and may posterity forget that ye were our countrymen. — Samuel Adams*

Samuel Adams speaks of the American Revolution, but the principle holds for the Christian as well. You're either engaged or not — it's your choice. You don't have to be involved if you choose not to be, but isn't it better to be active for the Lord's work? It's not a "got to" but a "get to" — God doesn't need us, but credits us for actions we couldn't do without Him anyway.

Know this, if you choose to engage, it's rough sometimes. Why are we surprised if the enemy fights back? That's the reason many Christians don't become involved; service for God is tough. It's easy to be discouraged. Battles are tough, and people want to quit. Be stubborn, and recall Paul's words in Ephesians 6 to be strong — it's a command to *stand your ground*.

You can choose to engage or not, but don't fall for the trap the world in which we live should be the priority — after all, it's not the permanent world, as Paul said:

> *Behold, I show you a mystery; we shall not all sleep, but we shall all be changed, in a moment, in the twinkling of an eye, at the last trump; for the trumpet shall sound, and the dead shall be raised incorruptible, and we shall be changed.*
> 1 Corinthians 15:51-52

When tough times come know the certainty of the future and the good guys win. It may not appear like it right now, but the answers written in the back of the book (as any math student knows) show the correct answer. Go ahead and sneak a peak — the end events are certain. That's called perspective, and when you have it, you get the following:

## Chapter Ten

> *Therefore, my beloved brethren, be ye steadfast, unmovable, always abounding in the work of the Lord, forasmuch as ye know that your labor is not in vain in the Lord.*     1 Corinthians 15:58

Service is tough, but don't forget who you work for. Your labor is not in vain, even though you may never see results. What Paul states at the end of 1 Corinthians (translated "labor") isn't the effort and work you put into it, but rather the tribulations resulting *from* that work. Don't quit. Satan doesn't attack non-threats. If you're under attack, it could mean you're on the right path — enemies ignore military non-threats. If you want an easier life do nothing for the Lord, and Satan and his cohorts will (to a certain extent) leave you alone.

> *I ate no pleasant bread, neither came flesh nor wine in my mouth, neither did I anoint myself at all, till three whole weeks were fulfilled.*     Daniel 10:3

Different kinds of fasts exist — Daniel denies himself the finer foods and drink, but does not completely eliminate food as fasting should prioritize the spiritual over physical. It's not making yourself holy, or scoring points with God, fasting adjusts your priorities — instead of feeding the flesh, you devote time to the Lord.

We take good care of our body — vitamins, organic food, avoiding preservatives and so on. Yet what about the spiritual side? It requires care as well. Is twice a week enough? What if you only fed your body twice a week? How long would your strength hold out? Your spiritual needs are no different and require feeding as well; fasting helps focus the priorities.

> *And in the four and twentieth day of the first month, as I was by the side of the great river, which is Hiddekel; then I lifted up mine eyes, and looked, and behold a certain man clothed in linen, whose loins were girded with fine gold of Uphaz:*
>     Daniel 10:4–5

The twentieth day of the first month is Nisan 24. The guy claiming to write Daniel specifies dates — if it was a late attempt at a forgery, why do this? Why open yourself up to scrutiny? As noted earlier, skeptics always attempt late-dating Daniel's book, as they believe the only way it's possible to be so accurate comes from writing *after* the events took place.

This description should sound familiar, but it's not from the book of Revelation.

> *His body also was like the beryl, and his face as the appearance of lightning, and his eyes as lamps of fire, and his arms and his feet like in color to polished brass, and the voice of his words like the voice of a multitude. And I Daniel alone saw the vision; for the men that were with me saw not the vision; but a great quaking fell upon them, so that they fled to hide themselves.*
>
> Daniel 10:6–7

Daniel has a similar experience to Paul on the Damascus road — those with him didn't see anything as the vision was private for Daniel alone.

> *Therefore I was left alone, and saw this great vision, and there remained no strength in me; for my comeliness was turned in me into corruption, and I retained no strength.*
>
> Daniel 10:8

A common response to seeing God or an angel as preconceived ideas melt and nothing remains but a feeling of inadequacy. Other examples in the Bible include:

- Luke 5:1–8 — Peter recognizes who Jesus is and says "Depart from me, for I am a sinful man"
- Revelation 1:9–18 — John the apostle.
- Isaiah 6:1–5 — After Isaiah sees the Lord, he proclaims "Woe is me, for I am undone, because I am a man of unclean lips."

> *Yet heard I the voice of his words; and when I heard the voice of his words, then was I in a deep sleep on my face, and my face toward the ground. And, behold, an hand touched me, which set me upon my knees and upon the palms of my hands. And he said unto me, O Daniel, a man greatly beloved, understand the words that I speak unto thee, and stand upright; for unto thee am I now sent. And when he had spoken this word unto me, I stood trembling.*
>
> Daniel 10:9–11

Who is this guy appearing to Daniel? Some commentators say Jesus, but he needs help as we'll see shortly, so don't confuse the previous guy with this angel.

> *Then said he unto me, fear not, Daniel; for from the first day that thou didst set thine heart to understand, and to chasten thyself before thy God, thy words were heard, and I am come for thy words.*
>
> Daniel 10:12

# Chapter Ten

The first day of prayer causes the dispatching of the answer, yet it didn't make it to Daniel immediately. Prayers *are* answered, but not always the *way* we want, and not always *when* we want. You're not granted three wishes from God as if He's a genie; you need patience and sometimes have to wait.

Answered prayer can be an enigma. Is the tumor malignant or benign? The prayers drift up to God, and we wait for the results. Heal now, Lord! Hear us! And the test comes back ... benign! Praise the Lord! God is Good! And on and on it goes.

Yet what if the test comes back malignant? Does the prayer chain celebrate and say God is good? Do people say "Praise the Lord?" Does the result change the goodness of God? Or did it only change our perception?

> *Content. That's the word. A state of heart in which you would be at peace if God gave you nothing more than he already has. Test yourself with this question: What if God's only gift to you were his grace to save you. Would you be content? You beg him to save the life of your child. You plead with him to keep your business afloat. You implore him to remove the cancer from your body. What if his answer is, "My grace is enough" Would you be content?*
>
> *You see, from heavens' perspective, grace is enough. If God did nothing more than save us from hell, could anyone complain? If God saved our souls and then left us to spend our lives leprosy-struck on a deserted island, would he be unjust? Having been given eternal life, dare we grumble at an aching body? Having been given heavenly riches, dare we bemoan earthly poverty?*
>
> *But there are those times when God, having given us his grace, hears our appeals and says, "My grace is sufficient for you." Is he being unfair?*\*

Prayer isn't our attempt to influence God to perform our bidding, rather the soldier reports for duty via prayer and makes himself available. Like any military, many times the private has no concept of the larger strategy. Sometimes we must live with the "no" answer, or a healing never taking place, or other events we don't understand. You have to lean on grace, and understand grace *is* enough.

---

\* Lucado (2005, page 131)

> *But the prince of the kingdom of Persia withstood me one and twenty days; but, lo, Michael, one of the chief princes, came to help me; and I remained there with the kings of Persia.*
>
> Daniel 10:13

The spiritual realm affects the physical and causes the spiritual angel to be delayed physically. It's an error to believe we live in the "real" world, and the spiritual world is "out there" somewhere. Not so. We inhabit at least ten dimensions, though we experience only four. What happens in those other six dimensions? Daniel 10 provides a glimpse. It's not "out there" somewhere, it's all around us.

Not convinced? Read 2 Kings chapter 6 as the Syrian army surrounds Elisha. As his servant wakes up seeing the Syrians he panics, but Elisha remains strangely calm. Why? He knows what really occurs in ten-dimensional space, while the servant does not. Elisha notices this guy's panic, and asks God to let the servant in on what Elisha already knows.

> *Therefore sent he thither horses, and chariots, and a great host; and they came by night, and compassed the city about. And when the servant of the man of God was risen early, and gone forth, behold, an host compassed the city both with horses and chariots. And his servant said unto him, Alas, my master! How shall we do? And he answered, Fear not; for they that be with us are more than they that be with them. And Elisha prayed, and said, LORD, I pray thee, open his eyes, that he may see. And the LORD opened the eyes of the young man; and he saw; and, behold, the mountain was full of horses and chariots of fire round about Elisha.*
>
> 2 Kings 6:14-17

A window into multi-dimensional spaces opens up, and the servant sees reality for the first time.

> *Now I am come to make thee understand what shall befall thy people in the latter days; for yet the vision is for many days.*
>
> Daniel 10:14

Amos 3:7 says "Surely the Lord God will do nothing, but he reveals his secret to his servants the prophets." God wants you to know — the future is certain, as well as *your* future. You may be discouraged or in despair in current circumstances, but end events are never in doubt.

# Chapter Ten

*For the Lord himself shall descend from heaven with a shout, with the voice of the archangel, and with the trump of God; and the dead in Christ shall rise first; Then we which are alive and remain shall be caught up together with them in the clouds, to meet the Lord in the air; and so shall we ever be with the Lord. Wherefore comfort one another with these words.*
1 Thessalonians 4:16-18

Why comfort? Because the end is sure. It doesn't matter how tough it is now, the end is sure, and near.

*And when he had spoken such words unto me, I set my face toward the ground, and I became dumb. And, behold, one like the similitude of the sons of men touched my lips; then I opened my mouth, and spoke, and said unto him that stood before me, O my lord, by the vision my sorrows are turned upon me, and I have retained no strength. For how can the servant of this my lord talk with this my lord? For as for me, straightway there remained no strength in me, neither is there breath left in me.*
Daniel 10:15-17

Daniel's in a tough spot and needs encouragement. A pattern repeating itself through the Bible (and our lives as well). Sometimes circumstances seem overwhelming and hopeless, requiring God to intervene for encouragement.

*Then there came again and touched me one like the appearance of a man, and he strengthened me, and said, O man greatly beloved, fear not; peace be unto thee, be strong, yea, be strong. And when he had spoken unto me, I was strengthened, and said, Let my lord speak; for thou hast strengthened me.*
Daniel 10:18-19

It's easy to become discouraged as the battle rages, and you have no idea where events lead. But persevere. Think of Paul — boy did he have troubles! Beaten, stoned (with rocks), and you always had to ask your travel agent when booking a cruise to make sure Paul wasn't on board — his ships always went down. Through all this Paul wasn't super-human. Sometimes he despaired of life (2 Corinthians 1). Yet Paul didn't quit, and stayed the course; at the end of his life he told Timothy "I have fought the good fight, I have finished my course, I have kept the faith."

*I will lift up mine eyes unto the hills, from whence cometh my help. My help cometh from the LORD, which made heaven and earth. He will not suffer thy foot to be moved; he that keepeth thee will not slumber. Behold, he that keepeth Israel shall neither slumber nor sleep. The LORD is thy keeper; the LORD is thy shade upon thy right hand. The sun shall not smite thee by day, nor the moon by night. The LORD shall preserve thee from all evil; he shall preserve thy soul. The LORD shall preserve thy going out and thy coming in from this time forth, and even for evermore.*   Psalm 121

He doesn't promise long life, or an easy journey.

*Then said he, Knowest thou why I come unto thee? And now will I return to fight with the prince of Persia; and when I am gone forth, lo, the prince of Greece shall come. But I will show thee that which is noted in the scripture of truth; and there is none that holdeth with me in these things, but Michael your prince.*   Daniel 10:20-21

We have the bizarre idea this world we live in is "real," but the real reality is quite different; recall Peter says all this disappears in one giant nuclear explosion. According to this chapter, countries have spiritual leaders behind them. The battle surrounds us — you're either involved or a casualty because you're on the battlefield behind enemy lines. If you haven't studied the armor of God in Ephesians 6, begin study and practice now.

*But now thus saith the LORD that created thee, O Jacob, and he that formed thee, O Israel, Fear not; for I have redeemed thee, I have called thee by thy name; thou art mine. When thou passest through the waters, I will be with thee; and through the rivers, they shall not overflow thee; when thou walkest through the fire, thou shalt not be burned; neither shall the flame kindle upon thee.*   Isaiah 43:1-2

*Chapter 13*

# Chapter Eleven

ONE OF THE REASONS CRITICS ATTACK Daniel with such voracity stems from this chapter and its clear prophecy (if you need a review of the attacks on Daniel return to the introduction and chapter 1). But even critics admit the accuracy of this chapter — that's why they "late date" the book after the events Daniel foretells. The translation of the Septuagint occurred sometime in the middle of this chapter, so a problem exists with their scholarship (no matter, don't let a little thing like facts get in the way).

But for normal people, this chapter reads exactly as claimed — prophecy of future governments and rulers; it breaks down into three sections.

1. The past — Verses 1–20.
2. Dual-fulfillment — Verses 21–35.
3. Obviously future — Verses 36–45.

Since the first twenty verses relate already fulfilled prophecy (and we're not history buffs), we'll skip some history (the NIV commentary contains good notes, as well as J Vernon McGee for those who like to dig into historical detail). When presented with this much historical account, two ways exist to deal with it — in exquisite detail over many pages, or approximate. We're not much into history for history's sake (since history records the fulfillment of the prophecy), so we'll skip some detail you can dig out for yourself. Some dates might vary by a few years; we'll use approximations as we're interested in understanding the flavor of the chapter, not a rigorous historical examination.

*Also I in the first year of Darius the Mede, even I, stood to confirm and to strengthen him. And now will I show thee the truth. Behold, there shall stand up yet three kings in Persia; and the fourth shall be far richer than they all; and by his strength through his riches he shall stir up all against the realm of Greece.*  Daniel 11:1-2

Xerxes appears fourth (485–465 BC) attacking Greece in 480 BC (many believe Xerxes appears in the Book of Esther as Ahasuerus). The attack leaves hard feelings with the Greeks, leading to the rise of Alexander the Great.

*And a mighty king shall stand up, that shall rule with great dominion, and do according to his will.*  Daniel 11:3

Alexander of Greece (335 BC) conquers Persia and the rest of the world, spreading the Greek language over the known world. God gets his work done — even using pagan kings. Having a common language becomes a significant advantage for Paul and the New Testament writers as they spread the gospel.

*And when he shall stand up, his kingdom shall be broken, and shall be divided toward the four winds of heaven; and not to his posterity, nor according to his dominion which he ruled; for his kingdom shall be plucked up, even for others beside those.*  Daniel 11:4

Alexander died without an heir in 323 BC; his four generals divide up the kingdom, but end up fighting among themselves. The two we're interested in are Ptolemy in Egypt, and Seleucus Nicator in Syria. These two can create confusion, so you'll quickly see why we've dispensed with absolute historical analysis.

*And the king of the south shall be strong, and one of his princes; and he shall be strong above him, and have dominion; his dominion shall be a great dominion.*  Daniel 11:5

Ptolemy I rules in the south while Seleucus Nicator rules Syria (the King of the north). These two and their descendants continue fighting for about 150 years; a battle with modern-day politics, marriages of convenience and power, deception, lies, murder, slander, and so on.

## Chapter Eleven

*And in the end of years they shall join themselves together; for the king's daughter of the south shall come to the king of the north to make an agreement; but she shall not retain the power of the arm; neither shall he stand, nor his arm; but she shall be given up, and they that brought her, and he that begat her, and he that strengthened her in these times.*   Daniel 11:6

Now things get strange, with arranged marriages and such. There's murder, divorce, and intrigue — politics as usual. The King takes an arranged wife for political reasons, divorces his existing wife, then she's spurned and exacts revenge on him later. But with Egypt and Syria fighting, who's caught in the middle? Israel. They get trampled as armies travel through their land on their north and south routes.

It's roughly in this period (to have a flavor of dates) the translation of the Septuagint occurs which contains Daniel. The critics have a problem and they'll have to argue the Septuagint wasn't really translated when it claims to be.

*But out of a branch of her roots shall one stand up in his estate, which shall come with an army, and shall enter into the fortress of the king of the north, and shall deal against them, and shall prevail; And shall also carry captives into Egypt their gods, with their princes, and with their precious vessels of silver and of gold; and he shall continue more years than the king of the north.*   Daniel 11:7-8

The arranged marriage and murders leave hard feelings, so Egypt attacks the north and wins, taking considerable loot back to Egypt.

*So the king of the south shall come into his kingdom, and shall return into his own land. But his sons shall be stirred up, and shall assemble a multitude of great forces; and one shall certainly come, and overflow, and pass through; then shall he return, and be stirred up, even to his fortress.*   Daniel 11:9-10

Then the north attacks Egypt, but loses.

*And the king of the south shall be moved with anger, and shall come forth and fight with him, even with the king of the north; and he shall set forth a great multitude; but the multitude shall be given into his hand. And when he hath taken away the multitude, his heart shall be lifted up; and he shall cast down many ten thousands; but he shall not be strengthened by it.*   Daniel 11:11-12

Another battle as the south attacks Syria.

*For the king of the north shall return, and shall set forth a multitude greater than the former, and shall certainly come after certain years with a great army and with much riches. And in those times there shall many stand up against the king of the south; also the robbers of thy people shall exalt themselves to establish the vision; but they shall fall. So the king of the north shall come, and cast up a siege mound, and take the most fortified cities; and the arms of the south shall not withstand, neither his chosen people, neither shall there be any strength to withstand. But he that cometh against him shall do according to his own will, and none shall stand before him; and he shall stand in the glorious land, which by his hand shall be consumed.*   Daniel 11:13-16

The glorious land is Israel. It's caught in the middle as armies trample through it.

*He shall also set his face to enter with the strength of his whole kingdom, and upright ones with him; thus shall he do; and he shall give him the daughter of women, corrupting her; but she shall not stand on his side, neither be for him.*   Daniel 11:17

Occurring in roughly 195 BC as Antiochus gives his daughter in marriage to Ptolemy, hoping her loyalty would corrupt the Egyptian kingdom (her name was Cleopatra). That didn't happen, as Cleopatra remains loyal to Egypt.

*After this shall he turn his face unto the coasts, and shall take many; but a prince for his own behalf shall cause the reproach offered by him to cease; without his own reproach he shall cause it to turn upon him. Then he shall turn his face toward the fortresses of his own land, but he shall stumble and fall, and not be found. Then shall stand up in his estate a raiser of taxes in the glory of the kingdom; but within few days he shall be destroyed, neither in anger, nor in battle.*   Daniel 11:18-20

Now the prophecy moves into a gray area, with some arguing it's historical, others yet future. Verses 21-35 deal with Antiochus Epiphanes, which we've seen in the past (chapter 8). Scholars debate if it's about him or the Antichrist, but as we've seen in the past, it's both.

> *And in his estate shall stand up a vile person, to whom they shall not give the honor of the kingdom; but he shall come in peaceably, and obtain the kingdom by flatteries. And with the arms of a flood shall they be overflown from before him, and shall be broken; yea, also the prince of the covenant.*
> Daniel 11:21-22

Antiochus Epiphanes comes to power in 175 BC. Beware those coming peaceably, using stealth, flattery, and telling you what you want to hear. Don't be afraid to speak the truth. Telling people what they want to hear instead of the truth isn't love — sometimes truth is hard.

Satan never appears in a red suit with a pitchfork. He comes in stealth and deceives you. That's the nature of deception — if you recognize it, you won't be deceived. Fooling the masses remains (and always has been) a simple task — tell the people what they want. Make the trains run on time and you can take over (in politics or the church). It's all what can you do for me, right now (as long as someone else pays for it).

The Antichrist himself comes in peace — for 3 ½ years it's pretty good.

> *And after the league made with him he shall work deceitfully; for he shall come up, and shall become strong with a small people. He shall enter peaceably even upon the fattest places of the province; and he shall do that which his fathers have not done, nor his fathers' fathers; he shall scatter among them the prey, and spoil, and riches; yea, and he shall plot his devices against the strong holds, even for a time.* Daniel 11:23-24

His time is limited. There will be an end.

> *And he shall stir up his power and his courage against the king of the south with a great army; and the king of the south shall be stirred up to battle with a very great and mighty army; but he shall not stand; for they shall plot against him. Yea, they that feed of the portion of his food shall destroy him, and his army shall overflow, and many shall fall down slain. And both these kings' hearts shall be to do mischief, and they shall speak lies at one table; but it shall not prosper; for yet the end shall be at the time appointed. Then shall he return into his*

*land with great riches; and his heart shall be against the holy covenant; and he shall do exploits, and return to his own land.*
Daniel 11:25-28

The end occurs at the appointed time with everything according to God's plan. Antiochus was a bad guy, but he worked according to God's plan (Romans 8:28).

*At the time appointed he shall return, and come toward the south; but it shall not be as the former, or as the latter. For the ships of Kittim shall come against him; therefore he shall be grieved, and return, and have indignation against the holy covenant; so shall he do; he shall even return, and have intelligence with them that forsake the holy covenant.*
Daniel 11:29-30

Rome helps defeat Antiochus. He returns to his land, taking out his frustration on the Jews about 170 BC.

*And forces shall stand on his part, and they shall pollute the sanctuary of strength, and shall take away the daily sacrifice, and they shall place the abomination that maketh desolate.*
Daniel 11:31

The abomination of desolation — sacrificing a pig on the altar and putting a statue of Zeus (or Jupiter) in the temple. Naturally this defiles the temple, and the Jews finally have enough of Antiochus' abuse.

*And such as do wickedly against the covenant shall he corrupt by flatteries; but the people that do know their God shall be strong, and do exploits.*
Daniel 11:32

Remember Daniel 6 — how did Daniel's enemies con the King to throw Daniel in the lion's den? Flattery. Appealing to pride to someone lacking a firm foundation works. A double-minded man is unstable (James 1:8), and becomes easily swayed by arguments appealing to his flesh, not logical analysis.

God's people perish for lack of knowledge (Hosea 4:6). Sadly, many pulpits don't teach the Word of God, instead giving people "seeker-friendly" churches and potlucks, while omitting sin, salvation and hell (after all, we don't want to offend anyone) while people perish for lack of proper instruction. How many teach the Bible? How many prepare the Christian to battle with the armor of God? The Christian lives in enemy territory, behind enemy lines and must be prepared for battle.

One question for those concerning themselves with potlucks and politics over the Bible — when did the Word of God become insufficient When did potlucks replace Jesus? When did God lose His power? When did salvation become Jesus plus?

As a result, many people sit in pews not knowing the Bible, and that's the fault of pastors. All churches should teach through the *entire* Bible; why some don't is a mystery. If people don't understand the Word of God, they're easy prey for the enemy to pick off as they have no foundation and no means to defend themselves. In contrast, people knowing their God shall be strong. Faith comes by hearing, and hearing by the Word of God (Romans 10:17).

> *And they that understand among the people shall instruct many; yet they shall fall by the sword, and by flame, by captivity, and by spoil, many days.* Daniel 11:33

God always preserves a remnant. In historical context, Daniel relates the Maccabeean revolt, told in 1 Maccabees chapter 2 (while not inspired scripture, it's useful for historical records).

> *Now when they shall fall, they shall be helped with a little help; but many shall cling to them with flatteries. And some of them of understanding shall fall, to test them, and to purge, and to make them white, even to the time of the end; because it is yet for a time appointed.* Daniel 11:34-35

A remnant always remains, no matter how bad things get. Elijah believed all were gone, but God saves 7,000 who didn't bow to Baal. Earlier in Daniel, all bowed but three Hebrew teenagers. In Revelation, God seals 144,000 Jews. God always preserves a group. It's easy to arrive to a point of hopelessness and despair as we look around, but learn the lesson from the Bible — God *always* preserves a remnant; don't fall for the lie nobody remains devoted to God.

Now we move to the final section of the vision contained in chapters 10-12; verse 36 forward obviously relates end-times prophecy and yet future.

> *And the king shall do according to his will; and he shall exalt himself, and magnify himself above every god, and shall speak marvelous things against the God of gods, and shall*

> *prosper till the indignation be accomplished; for that that is determined shall be done.*
> Daniel 11:36

Antiochus didn't do this, so it remains a future event yet to occur (he placed an image of Zeus, not himself, in the temple). What has been determined shall be done. If you watched the ten commandments on TV, you recall the famous Egyptian saying "So it is written, so it shall be." The future is certain, and the answers are in the back of the book.

> *Neither shall he regard the gods of his fathers, nor the desire of women, nor regard any god; for he shall magnify himself above all.*
> Daniel 11:37

God of his fathers — could he be Jewish? The Gentiles worshiped anything and everything, not having a consistent god.

Some mistake the phrase "desire of women" to mean something it's not — the desire of all Jewish women was to bear the Messiah (which implies a Jewish background). Whether this guy turns out to be Jewish or not becomes a matter of intense debate among scholars and won't be settled. But he won't regard any god, which implies one world religion and gives credence to those arguing against the scholars holding the Jewish background existing in this verse. Which group of scholars is correct? We'll wait and see, even though the church won't be around to see it.

> *But in his estate shall he honor the God of fortresses; and a god whom his fathers knew not shall he honor with gold, and silver, and with precious stones, and pleasant things. Thus shall he do in the strongest fortresses with a foreign god, whom he shall acknowledge and increase with glory; and he shall cause them to rule over many, and shall divide the land for gain.*
> Daniel 11:38–39

His rule does not last long (less than seven years).

> *And at the time of the end shall the king of the south push at him; and the king of the north shall come against him like a whirlwind, with chariots, and with horsemen, and with many ships; and he shall enter into the countries, and shall overflow and pass through. He shall enter also into the glorious land, and many countries shall be overthrown, but these shall escape out of his hand, even Edom, and Moab, and the chief of the children of Ammon.*
> Daniel 11:40–41

Why do these escape? So the Jewish remnant has somewhere to flee; some areas escape the Antichrist's control.

> *He shall stretch forth his hand also upon the countries, and the land of Egypt shall not escape. But he shall have power over the treasures of gold and of silver, and over all the precious things of Egypt; and the Libyans and the Ethiopians shall be at his steps. But tidings out of the east and out of the north shall trouble him; therefore he shall go forth with great fury to destroy, and utterly to sweep away many. And he shall plant the tabernacles of his palace between the seas in the glorious holy mountain; yet he shall come to his end, and none shall help him.*   Daniel 11:42–45

Antichrist comes to his end, with nobody helping him as Satan's best shot ends in defeat, and he knows it.

Chapter 12 of Daniel contains the finale — do you want to know the end of times? Stick around for the end, as everyone knows the answers appear in the back of the book.

*Chapter* 14

# Chapter Twelve

CHAPTERS 10–12 OF DANIEL MUST BE VIEWED as one unit (chapter breaks in the Bible appear at times rather arbitrarily, occurring in unfortunate places). Recall back in chapter 10 verse 14 — the prophecy concerns Daniel's people, i.e. the Jews — it's not the church — an idea becoming critical when you study Revelation or grave mistakes can be made.

> *And at that time shall Michael stand up, the great prince which standeth for the children of thy people, and there shall be a time of trouble, such as never was since there was a nation even to that same time; and at that time thy people shall be delivered, every one that shall be found written in the book.*
> Daniel 12:1

The end is certain; a time arrives making $5 gas appear trivial. The church won't be here during the great tribulation, but don't make the mistake it's easy-going until then. Daniel speaks of *the* great tribulation (note the definite article) pointing to a specific event, but considerable great tribulation exists until then, as most of the church experienced for most of the last two thousand years.

Society has not improved with time — entropy says the universe moves toward chaos and disorder. But at that time, "thy people" (the Jews) shall be delivered.

> *And many of them that sleep in the dust of the earth shall awake, some to everlasting life, and some to shame and everlasting contempt. And they that be wise shall shine as the brightness of the firmament; and they that turn many to righteousness as the stars for ever and ever.*    Daniel 12:2-3

You are eternal whether you want to be or not, but you have the option of where you spend it. All paths really do lead to God, but where you go after that isn't so certain (see Revelation 20:11-15 and the great white throne judgment).

> *But thou, O Daniel, shut up the words, and seal the book, even to the time of the end; many shall run to and fro, and knowledge shall be increased.* Daniel 12:4

Many misunderstood this verse to imply a general increase in knowledge, which we've seen. From the moon landing in the 1960s until today, knowledge increases by orders of magnitude — it's a geometric progression. But that's not what Daniel has in mind.

The knowledge in view concerns the Bible and prophecy; many times we don't understand until later. For example, the prophecies saying Israel would reclaim their land have been allegorized as people had no concept Israel could ever regain the Biblical land. Today it's old news, as on May 14 1948 they've been re-gathered in the land as the Bible said. It's not an allegory, it meant what it said.

In a similar vein, the to and fro mentioned does not imply flying on airplanes across the globe. No, the angel means travel through the Bible looking for answers as people begin to realize it means what it says.

> *Behold, the days come, saith the Lord GOD, that I will send a famine in the land, not a famine of bread, nor a thirst for water, but of hearing the words of the LORD.* Amos 8:11

Everyone today wants to understand the end times; even secular people study it. But not many find the answer they want. Whenever conflict flares up in the Middle East experts come out wondering "is this Armageddon?" As the final days approach, it's *knowledge of the Bible* which increases. For example, consider the following.

> *This then is the message which we have heard of him, and declare unto you, that **God is light**, and in him is no darkness at all.* 1 John 1:5

The Greek word for light is "Phos" — meaning never kindled and therefore never quenched*. God *is* light. Not light-like, or

---

\*   Zodhiates (1992b, page 945)

having the characteristics of light. That should bother you. Why? Something called the two-slit experiment and wave-particle duality of light.

Still not bothered? God is a trinity. But if God is light, and light is a duality, we've got problems. The Bible has an error! Whenever you think a problem exists, it's a lack of understanding, and a chance for God to reveal to you something you don't have right now — fulfilling Daniel's writing knowledge will increase. This might keep you up at night, but only until the Holy Spirit provides the answer, which He does back in John's gospel.

> *Nevertheless when he, the Spirit of truth, is come, he will guide you into all truth; for* **he shall not speak of himself***; but whatsoever he shall hear, that shall he speak; and he will show you things to come. He shall glorify me; for he shall receive of mine, and shall show it unto you.* John 16:13-14

"He shall not speak of Himself" — and that's the answer. Based on these passages light contains another characteristic besides particle or wave physicists working on the theory of everything (string theory) should look for. But they can't find it experimentally because it always appears as either a wave or particle, for the Holy Spirit never speaks of Himself — the third manifestation of light will be difficult to find experimentally, but the effects will be felt by indirect means.

Much like the quantum breakthrough in the early 1900s which took physicists on a different (and correct) path, physicists today working on new theories should consider another characteristic of light. It's there, but difficult to detect. Naturally, we didn't even know this problem until 1900 — but John wrote the answer in the first century, while knowledge took time to catch up to revelation.

The Holy Spirit never speaks of Himself, acting like a gentleman rather than a bully forcing you into a position. That's the danger of some of the strange doctrine focusing exclusively on the Holy Spirit; He doesn't speak of Himself, but testifies of Jesus.

> *Then I Daniel looked, and, behold, there stood two others, the one on this side of the bank of the river, and the other on that side of the bank of the river. And one said to the man clothed in linen, which was above the waters of the river, How long shall it be to the end of these wonders?* Daniel 12:5-6

Jesus appears back in chapter 10 as the guy in linen. But the question is, when? That's what we always want to know. The disciples in Matthew 24 ask, when will these things be? Not exactly troubled by the events themselves, they're only concerned with *when* those events occur.

> *And I heard the man clothed in linen, which was above the waters of the river, when he held up his right hand and his left hand unto heaven, and swore by him that liveth for ever that it shall be for a time, times, and an half; and when he shall have accomplished the breaking up of the power of the holy people, all these things shall be finished.* Daniel 12:7

Times is a dual, like "both." Thus you have three and one-half years once again as the Bible speaks of the great tribulation in several ways, but always referring to the same period of time.

- 42 months — Revelation 11:2,13:5
- 1,260 days — Revelation 11:3,12:6
- Half of one week (literally "sevens") — Daniel 9:27
- Times, time and half a time — Daniel 12:7

The seven-year duration of the tribulation isn't exactly true — the 70th week of Daniel spans seven years, but the first half (after the rapture) works out fairly well. But you don't want to be around for the last half as judgment descends on a world refusing to acknowledge God. It's time to acknowledge prophecy as literal. What other interval could God have used to emphasize the point? The seventy weeks of Daniel represent an exact literal period of time.

> *And I heard, but I understood not. Then said I, O my Lord, what shall be the end of these things?* Daniel 12:8

So if the vision causes Daniel confusion, don't be surprised if it equally confuses us. These are end-times events; some are clear, others aren't. Some we understand now, others not.

> *And he said, Go thy way, Daniel; for the words are closed up and sealed till the time of the end. Many shall be purified, and made white, and tested; but the wicked shall do wickedly; and none of the wicked shall understand; but the wise shall understand.* Daniel 12:9-10

The closer to the end we travel, the more understanding we see. Don't be surprised if your unsaved friends don't understand for the natural man can't understand because they are spiritually discerned — they are foolishness to him.

## Chapter Twelve

*And from the time that the daily sacrifice shall be taken away, and the abomination that maketh desolate set up, there shall be a thousand two hundred and ninety days.* Daniel 12:11

Why the extra thirty days? We don't know. Most speculate either the great white throne judgment occurs during this time or it's setting up for the millennium rule of Christ. But we don't know.

*Blessed is he that waiteth, and cometh to the thousand three hundred and five and thirty days. But go thou thy way till the end be; for thou shalt rest, and stand in thy lot at the end of the days.* Daniel 12:12-13

Same problem as the previous verse; we don't know what this period relates to. Daniel will die, but note the resurrection promise at the end. And thus ends Daniel's book, with the promise of the resurrection.

A final summary of Daniel's character appears in Weirsbe's commentary (page 308–311).

- *He believed in a sovereign God.*
- *He had a disciplined prayer life.*
- *He studied the Word of God and believed it.*
- *He had an understanding of spiritual warfare.*
- *He sought only to glorify God.*
- *He realized that he had a work to do.*
- *He was tactful and considerate.*
- *He had insight into human history.*
- *He lived up to his name (God is my judge).*

*Daniel's book contains much more than simple Sunday School stories in flannel. His life not only provides examples for us, the stories also contain lessons for what* not *to do, as various other characters make mistakes we should learn from. Finally, Daniel provides views of end-time events we must study and be aware of, as the Lord desires none to be fearful of future events.*

*Appendix A*

---

# The Confusion of Religion

---

CONTRARY TO THE POPULAR TEACHING OF value relativism, right and wrong *do* exist — even fake TV Characters know it.

> *Right and wrong do exist. Just because you don't know what the right answer is—maybe there's even no way you could know what the right answer is—doesn't make your answer right or even okay. It's much simpler than that. It's just plain wrong.*
> "House" — Season One, Episode 121 "Three Stories"

In medicine, you're either right or wrong. Heal the patient or kill him. No middle ground exists, no passing the buck, no value relativism, no "objective truth." Similarly in the game of Blackjack, for any given situation *one* correct move exists. Other possibilities may work out once in a while, but that's luck, not sound analysis.

So what absolute standard exists for the questions of life?

- Who am I?
- Why am I here?
- Where am I going?
- How did I get here?

If you're looking at candidate solutions, they must provide answers to *all* these questions. Look for a religion answering *all* the basic questions, *while remaining internally consistent. If* a god exists, and *if* he's all-powerful, and *if* he transmitted a message to us, it must be consistent, must it not? Thus if a candidate religion contains obvious falsehoods it must be eliminated from contention.

The question remains — who is Jesus? A question always dividing — it's acceptable to discuss god, religion and any other topic, but ask about Jesus and people get uneasy. It's where religions diverge; both Mormons and Jehovah Witnesses (among others) reject the deity of Jesus (He's not God). That's a position you're free to accept or reject as you wish, but you'll quickly notice it creates problems with other positions those groups claim to hold (and opposing claims can't *all* be correct).

First, find out who God is. Consider the following passage, and ask yourself who Isaiah speaks about.

> *In the year that king Uzziah died I saw also the Lord sitting upon a throne, high and lifted up, and his train filled the temple. Above it stood the seraphim: each one had six wings; with two he covered his face, and with two he covered his feet, and with two he did fly. And one cried unto another, and said, Holy, holy, holy, is the Lord of hosts: the whole earth is full of his glory. And the posts of the door moved at the voice of him that cried, and the house was filled with smoke. Then said I, Woe is me! for I am undone; because I am a man of unclean lips, and I dwell in the midst of a people of unclean lips: for mine eyes have seen the King, the Lord of hosts.* Isaiah 6:1-5

That's Jehovah God they'll say. No disagreement exists on that passage — it's the Lord (Jehovah, God) Isaiah sees. Now consider a passage in John:

> *But though he had done so many miracles before them, yet they believed not on him; That the saying of Isaiah the prophet might be fulfilled, which he spoke, Lord, who hath believed our report? And to whom hath the arm of the Lord been revealed? Therefore they could not believe, because that Isaiah said again, He hath blinded their eyes, and hardened their heart; that they should not see with their eyes, nor understand with their heart, and be converted, and I should heal them. These things said Isaiah, when he saw his glory, and spoke of him.* John 12:37-41

Pronouns fill this passage, dig for yourself and determine who they refer to (we'll wait). Notice "he" refers to Jesus — no disagreement should exist here either. The context of the passage is clear "though he had done so many miracles before them" — the "he" is Jesus. Right?

Some groups state Jesus isn't God — a perfectly reasonable hypothesis requiring further analysis. The truth or falsity isn't important (and we're not going to enter the discussion here), because *for our purposes it doesn't matter.* What *does* matter is Mormons, Jehovah Witnesses, and other groups, while claiming Jesus isn't God, *do* claim to accept the Bible as the authoritative Word of God.

And that's when problems begin.

Your bible likely notes John chapter 12 verse 41 alludes to Isaiah 6 — "These things said Isaiah, when he saw his glory, and spoke of him" (replacing the pronouns, "These things said Isaiah, when Isaiah saw Jehovah's glory, and spoke of Jehovah"). And who (we've agreed) does Isaiah speak of in chapter 6? Jehovah God! John (we've agreed) discusses Jesus, so Isaiah saw the glory of Jesus and was God (Jehovah, Father God). So ... wait for it ... Jesus *is* God.

You might not like that example or rationalize it away (Chuck Missler says never underestimate a humans ability to rationalize), so consider other famous passages.

> *Who hath wrought and done it, calling the generations from the beginning? I the Lord, the first, and with the last; I am he.*
> Isaiah 41:4

Who is the first and last? Jehovah God, right?

> *Thus saith the Lord the King of Israel, and his redeemer the Lord of hosts; I am the first, and I am the last; and beside me there is no God.*
> Isaiah 4:6

Who is the first and last? Jehovah God, right?

> *"I am Alpha and Omega, the beginning and the ending," saith the Lord, "which is, and which was, and which is to come, the Almighty."*
> Revelation 1:8

Who is the Alpha and Omega, first and last, beginning and end? Jehovah God, right?

> *Saying, "I am Alpha and Omega, the first and the last: and, What thou seest, write in a book, and send it unto the seven churches which are in Asia; unto Ephesus, and unto Smyrna, and unto Pergamos, and unto Thyatira, and unto Sardis, and unto Philadelphia, and unto Laodicea."*
> Revelation 1:11

Who is the Alpha and Omega, first and last, beginning and end? Jehovah God, right? Notice a pattern here? God is the first and last, beginning and end, alpha and omega — all express the same idea. It's Jehovah God, the Father, the eternal God, or however you want to express it. We'll consider one more verse.

> *And when I saw him, I fell at his feet as dead. And he laid his right hand upon me, saying unto me, "Fear not; I am the first and the last:" "I am he that liveth, and was dead; and, behold, I am alive for evermore, Amen; and have the keys of hell and of death."* Revelation 1:17–18

Who is the first and last? Jehovah God! But wait, he was living, then dead, now alive for evermore? That only fits Jesus. Jesus is God. Period. If you want to dig into this more yourself, examine verse 5 of Revelation chapter 1 where the later pronouns refer to — it's Jesus Christ. Mentioned in chapter 1 are John, Jesus, and God. So even in verses 8 and 11, the pronoun refers to Jesus, and in red-letter Bibles appears in Red to indicate it's words of Jesus.

Once again, you're free to disagree Jesus is God if you wish, you're free to reject the Bible, you're free to believe the moon is made of cheese, you're free to believe anything you want; nothing is in jeopardy here, and we're not in any way telling you to believe one way or the other — believe as you will — we're just giving you something to think about in the spirit of open discussion.

However, *if* you state Jesus isn't God, *and* claim you accept the Bible as the authoritative Word of God, massive contradictions arise. To escape this paradox you must state the Bible isn't authoritative, and not all of it is true. Otherwise you've got big problems in river city — something doesn't fit as two contradictory positions can't *both* be correct. Which is it? Is the Bible correct, or extra-Biblical teaching? It's your choice, but consider what Paul said in Galatians.

> *I marvel that ye are so soon removed from him that called you into the grace of Christ unto another gospel: Which is not another; but there be some that trouble you, and would pervert the gospel of Christ. But **though we, or an angel from heaven, preach any other gospel unto you than that which we have preached unto you, let him be accursed**. As we said before, so say I now again, If any man preach any other gospel unto you than that ye have received, let him be accursed.* Galatians 1:6–9

# The Confusion of Religion

When groups disagree with the Bible (Jesus is not God) you have a choice — either they're right, or the Bible is. We're not even entering into a discussion of *which* is correct, as for this point *it doesn't matter* — only one *can* be correct, a problem illustrated by the following. Suppose person "A" says the sky is orange, while person "B" says the sky is purple. What possibilities exist?

- "A" is right and "B" is wrong.
- "A is wrong and "B" is right.
- Both "A" and "B" are wrong.

But note, *they can't both be right*. Thus, if the Bible states Jesus is God, and yet a group maintains Jesus isn't God while accepting the authority of the Bible, that makes no sense as both "A" and "B" can not be right — it's not possible (at most one is correct, or they're both wrong). You can choose which you wish to believe, but you encounter a hopeless paradox attempting to force contradictory ideas into agreement.

Another issue presents itself best illustrated by a Jon Courson story. Suppose you're in church minding your own business. Suddenly a person comes in wearing a long trench-coat, acting quite suspicious. He opens his coat, tosses in a grenade, and walks out. Everyone freezes. But one person springs into action, grabbing the little old lady sitting next to him, throws her on the grenade before it explodes, saving everyone.

What would you think? Sure, he saved everyone, but why did he force someone else to do something he himself was unwilling to do? That's not fair!

Exactly. And yet if Jesus isn't God, the same situation exists — God created something to do the job He was unwilling to do. What kind of God is that?

Too much confusion and hostility exists over religion — you're free to believe *whatever* you want, and should be respectful of other opinions differing from yours. Tolerance doesn't mean you won't be exposed to different views, but it does mean civilized debate and discussion should ensue as civilized discussion is the hallmark of true tolerance, not the shouting down and silencing of people holding different views.

You can believe the Bible is the Word of God or not. Your choice. You can believe Jesus is God or not. Your choice. But know what you believe, and why.

... and make sure your candidate religion answers *all* the foundational questions of life.

# References

Alexander (1999). *Zondervan Handbook to the Bible.* Zondervan Publishing House.

Anonymous (2021). Unperson. *Wikipedia* https://web.archive.org/web/20211006190304/https://simple.m.wikipedia.org/wiki/Unperson. Accessed 2012-12-12.

Epstein, D. M. (2008). Excerpt: The Lincolns. *NPR* https://www.npr.org/templates/story/story.php?storyId=93255875. Accessed 2021-12-19.

Fisher, M. (1996). Stark prayer sparks an absolute political furor. *Washington Post* https://www.washingtonpost.com/archive/politics/1996/05/20/stark-prayer-sparks-an-absolute-political-furor/5e674306-da80-47d8-b0bc-b8cf4dbfbdfa/. Accessed 2021-12-20.

Josephus, F. (1987). *The Works of Josephus.* Hendrickson Publishers.

Lewis, C. (1990). *The Screwtape Letters.* Barbour and Company.

Lucado, M. (2005). *Thomas Nelson.* Thomas Nelson.

McGee, J. V. (1982). *Thru the Bible*, Volume III. Thomas Nelson.

Missler, C. (1991). *Daniel's 70 weeks (tapes with notes).* Koinonia House.

Orwell, G. (1949). *1984.* Harcourt Brace Jovanovich.

Reuters (2007). Kathy griffins jesus remark cut from emmy show. *Reuters* https://www.reuters.com/article/us-griffin-emmys-idUSN1144512920070911. Accessed 2021-12-14.

Taunton, L. (2007, 12). Richard Dawkins: The Atheist Evangelist. *byFaith* http://byfaithonline.com/richard-dawkins-the-atheist-evangelist/. Accessed 2012-07-19.

Times, N. (2007). Court splits abortion and fetus murder. *NY Times* https://www.nytimes.com/2007/11/23/us/23texas.html. Accessed 2021-12-18.

Zodhiates, S. (1992a). *The Complete Word Study Dictionary New Testament.* ANG International.

Zodhiates, S. (1992b). *The Complete Word Study New Testament.* ANG International.

www.ingramcontent.com/pod-product-compliance
Lightning Source LLC
Chambersburg PA
CBHW032039290426
44110CB00012B/878